The Dawning of Redemption

"The Pentateuch seems forbidding and alien to many believers. But Ian Vaillancourt has written a user-friendly introduction to the theology of the Pentateuch that will enable readers to get a big picture of the theology of the first five books of the Bible. He also shows in each chapter how the Pentateuch points forward to and is fulfilled in Jesus Christ. Readers will see more clearly how the entire Bible fits together in this fine work."

Thomas R. Schreiner, James Buchanan Harrison Professor of New Testament Interpretation, The Southern Baptist Theological Seminary

"You can't make sense of a musical if you don't hear the opening songs; you can't make sense of a book if you don't read the opening chapters; you can't make sense of a trial if you don't listen to the opening arguments; and in much the same way, you won't ever make sense of the Bible if you don't understand the themes of its opening books, the Pentateuch. What my friend Ian does so well in *The Dawning of Redemption* is introduce the major themes that begin at the beginning and extend all the way to the end. If you'll read it, you won't better understand just those five books, but also the sixty-one that follow. You'll better understand the Pentateuch, to be sure, but also the entire Bible."

Tim Challies, author, *Seasons of Sorrow: The Pain of Loss and the Comfort of God*

"An engaging, accessible entry into the five books that launch the story of the Bible. *The Dawning of Redemption* is sure to mobilize many in the church to dust off 'Moses's book' and see in its pages the opening act of a beautiful story of redemption."

Andrew Abernethy, Professor of Old Testament, Wheaton College; author, *Savoring Scripture*

"This wonderful introduction to the first five books of the Bible—the book of Moses—is popular-level, easy to read, and extremely helpful in putting the storyline together so that modern-day readers can appreciate material that seems otherwise irrelevant by today's standards. I wholeheartedly recommend this little volume to anyone interested in the Bible, whether as beginner or serious student. Readers will be assisted in understanding how these early parts of the Bible point forward to the coming of a redeemer, Jesus Christ."

Peter J. Gentry, Senior Professor of Old Testament, The Southern Baptist Theological Seminary; Distinguished Visiting Professor of Old Testament and Senior Research Fellow of the Text and Canon Institute, Phoenix Seminary

"Affirming the Pentateuch as Moses's book and as God's living word, Vaillancourt shows how the Bible's initial portrait of redemption foreshadows Christ's person and saving work. *The Dawning of Redemption* overviews nine stages in the Bible's opening story and at every point celebrates Christ as the climax of history, the substance of all shadows, and the bestower of restoration blessings. Vaillancourt rightly recognizes that the Pentateuch is Christian Scripture, and he clearly and faithfully invites new readers into the message of the Bible's first five books."

Jason S. DeRouchie, Research Professor of Old Testament and Biblical Theology, Midwestern Baptist Theological Seminary; Content Developer and Global Trainer, Hands to the Plow Ministries

The Dawning of Redemption

The Story of the Pentateuch and the Hope of the Gospel

Ian J. Vaillancourt

:: CROSSWAY®

WHEATON, ILLINOIS

Library of Congress Cataloging-in-Publication Data
Names: Vaillancourt, Ian J., author.
Title: The dawning of redemption : the story of the Pentateuch and the Hope of the Gospel / Ian J. Vaillancourt.
Description: Wheaton, Illinois : Crossway, 2022. | Includes bibliographical references and index.
Identifiers: LCCN 2022006066 (print) | LCCN 2022006067 (ebook) | ISBN 9781433581229 (trade paperback) | ISBN 9781433581236 (pdf) | ISBN 9781433581243 (mobipocket) | ISBN 9781433581250 (epub)
Subjects: LCSH: Bible. Pentateuch--Commentaries. | Redemption—Biblical teaching.
Classification: LCC BS1225.53 .V3355 2022 (print) | LCC BS1225.53 (ebook) | DDC 222/.107—dc23/
    eng/20220615
LC record available at https://lccn.loc.gov/2022006066
LC ebook record available at https://lccn.loc.gov/2022006067

Crossway is a publishing ministry of Good News Publishers.

BP			31	30	29	28	27	26	25	24	23	22
15	14	13	12	11	10	9	8	7	6	5	4	3	2	1

To
Caleb James Vaillancourt
and
Emily Karis Vaillancourt
As you continue to diligently seek the Lord, Mom and I pray that our great Redeemer and his glorious gospel would be your greatest life passions.

Contents

Preface

AS A WAY OF GETTING READERS on the same page, we are going to ask and answer four questions before we dive into the word of God. Here they are:

1. What does the word *Pentateuch* mean?
2. What does YHWH mean, and why does this vowel-free word appear so often in this book?
3. What does *torah* mean, and why does this italicized word appear so often in this book?
4. Which Bible version does this book primarily employ?

We'll briefly answer each of these questions in turn.

First, what does the word *Pentateuch* mean? Do not be embarrassed if you have never heard the word *Pentateuch*. If you have not, I'm glad you picked this book up, and I hope you read on. Simply put, *Pentateuch* is a fancy word of Greek origin that refers to the first five books of the Old Testament—Genesis, Exodus, Leviticus, Numbers, and Deuteronomy. It's as simple as that: the Pentateuch is the first five books of the Old Testament.

Second, what does YHWH mean? The personal name for God in the Old Testament is often spelled YHWH and pronounced Yahweh. Although most English Bibles use the title "the LORD" for this Hebrew word, in this book we will use YHWH, except when I am quoting from an English Bible. This will give readers practice: we can make the switch from "the LORD" to "YHWH" in our minds as we encounter Old Testament citations, and hopefully this new habit will spill over to our personal reading of the Old Testament.

Third, what does *torah* mean? *Torah* is a Hebrew word that is usually translated "law" in English Bibles. Since this word does not have an exact English equivalent, I will explain the word in the book and use *torah* or *instruction* instead of *law*, except when I am quoting from an English Bible. So when you encounter the word "law" in a direct citation of the Old Testament, I encourage you to supply "*torah*" or "instruction." This will help you remember that this Hebrew word means much more than our English word *law* usually calls to mind.

Fourth, which Bible version does this book primarily employ? Although there are many excellent English translations of the Bible, the essentially literal nature of the ESV is a bit more suited to a study like this one because it will help us notice details in God's word.

Acknowledgments

THIS BOOK COULD NOT have been written apart from the impact of many teachers, students, editors, friends, and family. When I first described the concept of this book to the editorial team at Crossway, I pointed to the authors who have especially shaped my understanding of the Pentateuch: John H. Sailhamer, Bruce K. Waltke, Stephen G. Dempster, Peter J. Gentry, Graeme Goldsworthy, Sidney Greidanus, T. Desmond Alexander, and L. Michael Morales. My desire was to write a short and understandable book that incorporated insights from these godly and insightful Old Testament scholars. Since beginning this project, I now joyfully add Sandra L. Richter as one who has had a particular shaping influence. Many of the strengths of this book are indebted to these scholars. Any shortcomings are, of course, my own.

This book also took shape through the Pentateuch course I teach at Heritage Theological Seminary in Cambridge, Ontario, Canada. The discipline of preparing this course helped to crystalize my thinking on this section of Scripture. Questions from my extremely insightful students over the years have sharpened my thinking in more ways than they know.

This book was also influenced by several discussions with Todd Augustine, director of acquisitions at Crossway. It has been a joy to work with an editor who is passionate about God's word and who is a relentless encourager of the authors under his care. When the editorial committee at Crossway approved my book proposal and offered me a publishing contract, Todd was not content to email me; he took the time to call so he could share the exciting news more personally. In the editing phase of production, Lydia Brownback helped with little tweaks to wording and lots of encouragement to the author, and these have resulted in a much stronger final manuscript. I am thankful to work with editors and a publisher who view their work as a ministry and who seek to glorify God in it.

As I was writing the initial chapters of this book, several friends took time to read them and provide feedback. These include Jacob and Roseanne Tomc, Brian Vautour, Andrew Hall, Nate and Jillian Amiri, Andrea Thom, and Natalie Vaillancourt. Their helpful feedback at the early stage of writing helped to refine those chapters, and also my approach to the rest of the book. Thank you! In addition, Jacob and Roseanne Tomc, Brian Vautour, Andrew Hall, Greg and Laura Vaillancourt, and Natalie Vaillancourt also read and gave feedback on the full manuscript when an initial draft was completed. My work is much stronger because of their insights. Once again, any shortcomings are my own.

Finally, I continue to praise God for the wonderful family he has blessed me with. Natalie and I are truly a team; the fabric of our lives has been woven together by the Lord, and everything either of us accomplishes is also the product of the other. Apart from the support and love of Natalie, the book you hold in your hands would not exist. I am also thankful for the wonderful teenaged kids we get to love and influence together—Caleb James and Emily Karis are greater blessings than we could have ever imagined. It is to them that this book is dedicated.

Ian J. Vaillancourt
Ancaster, Ontario
Spring 2022

Introduction

Getting Oriented to Moses's Book of Redemption

THE THEATER LIGHTS ARE DIM, and everyone's attention is fixed on the screen. Those watching are comfortable in their seats and so wrapped up in the story that popcorn sits uneaten on every lap. This is why no one really notices when, fifteen minutes into the action, we tiptoe in. We find a few seats in the back corner and begin to piece the story together. Twenty minutes pass, then thirty, then a full hour, and by the time the theater lights come back on, we have a nagging feeling that we are missing something. Sure, we *sort of* figured out the story's high points, but without its essential first part, we could not enjoy the movie the same way as everyone else.

This is a book about the essential first act of the Bible's story. We'll learn that if we are Christians who want to understand the gospel better, the Pentateuch is a great place to start. Although this might sound counterintuitive, it's true. As we go deeper in Genesis, Exodus, Leviticus, Numbers, and Deuteronomy, a black-and-white grasp of the Bible's message will increasingly give way to a vision of the gospel in resplendent color. These foundational books are the entry point into the biblical story that continues through the Old and New Testaments and gloriously concludes in the book of Revelation. Without the Pentateuch, there would be no first act in the grand drama. Apart from this portion of Scripture, we would have no basis for understanding how the world came into existence, our place in relation to the broader world, the reason we are inclined to sin against God and other people, the yearning in our hearts for something more, and the promise of God to intervene on our behalf. And these truths are found in the *first three chapters* of the Pentateuch.

As the Pentateuch continues, we encounter a God who makes glorious promises of salvation (e.g., Gen. 3:15), who judges those who reject him (e.g., Gen. 6), who guarantees salvation for his people by making covenants (e.g., Gen. 15), who is faithful even when his people are faithless (e.g., Gen. 16), who chooses to work through undeserving and imperfect people (e.g., Gen. 38), and who always works for the ultimate good of his people (e.g., Gen. 50:20). And these truths are found in the *first book* of the Pentateuch. Over four more books, the Pentateuch reveals more about God and his ways, builds on the biblical story, and sets us up for everything that follows.

Reading the Pentateuch can also be challenging because a lot of its content may *seem* unfit for contemporary application. In the Pentateuch we read of long lifespans, we find lengthy genealogies, and we encounter an extended description of how to build a tent dwelling for Israel's God. Although some of the instructions for community living are immediately applicable to our situation (e.g., "You shall not murder," Ex. 20:13), others seem so far removed from our day that we may ask ourselves why we need to read about them (e.g., laws about a goring ox in Ex. 21:28–32). If we are reading the Pentateuch because of an overriding conviction that Christians should be shaped by the *entire* Bible, perhaps it is tempting to be disengaged as we read these sections, or worse, to read with a sense of smug superiority over the characters in the drama. Neither of these options seems very edifying.

As the Pentateuch continues, the questions also continue. What are we to make of priests and animal sacrifices (the book of Leviticus)? What about the hesitance of a desert-dwelling nation to engage in a God-ordained holy war (the book of Numbers)? Although the book of Deuteronomy contains some immediately practical content, what are we to make of its instructions about the kind of king to set over Israel (Deut. 17:14–20), or its warnings about being cast out of the land of promise (Deut. 28:15–69)? Do any of these things have bearing on our twenty-first-century lives?

The best preparation to dig deeply in any section of the Bible is to gain a sense of the big picture. That is the purpose of this book: to give a big-picture sense of the story so readers will be equipped to dig into its details on their own. The Bible—from Genesis to Revelation—tells the story of a God who created the world with humanity as its crowning climax, of a people who chose to rebel against their Creator, and of a God who responded with a promise to rescue his creation. Since the stories of creation and the fall into sin are told in the first three chapters of Genesis, we can say that the rest of the Bible—from Genesis 3:15 to the end of Revelation—tells the story of God's rescue of rebels. The technical term for this rescue is *redemption*, and a little later in this introduction I will explain this word in more detail.

So the Bible tells the story of God's rescue of rebels—his redemption of sinners. In this book on the Pentateuch, we are going to help our understanding along by seeing this portion of Scripture as the first act in the Bible's grand story of redemption. Instead of focusing on minute details as a commentary would, we are going to get a sense of the whole—of the dawning of redemption as it unfolds in Genesis, Exodus, Leviticus, Numbers, and Deuteronomy. We will do this by unpacking nine key elements in the Pentateuch's storyline of redemption. As we understand these central concepts, we will be better equipped to read the details of these books on our own because we will be able to relate them to the larger story.

Before we dive into the nine themes of redemption, we will spend the rest of this introduction getting better oriented to the Pentateuch. We will think about the Pentateuch as a beautifully written historical document that is, first and foremost, the precious word of God. We will also think about the Pentateuch as authored by Moses, who wrote five books and one book at the same time. Next, we will gain a better understanding of the word *redemption* before we lay out a road map for the rest of this book. Finally, the introduction will conclude the same way every chapter will: by looking forward from the Pentateuch to Christ and by providing some discussion questions so you or your group can think through the material a little more.

The Pentateuch Is the Precious Word of God

Let's begin by imagining Moses: an eighty-year-old man from a nation of slaves had entered the most powerful throne room of his day. He was there with his spokesman brother to confront Pharaoh, the leader who had enslaved the Jews. Over the course of Moses's bold demands and ten horrendous plagues sent by his God, the Israelites were set free. Then when Pharaoh had second thoughts and pursued them with his army, YHWH caused the Red Sea to divide so that his people could pass through on dry land before those same walls of water engulfed their pursuers. What a scene!

As we picture it, we might even feel as though we are missing out, as though our experience of God would be stronger if only we had been there to witness even some of these events.

Although I agree that it would have been awesome to witness these events as they unfolded, we need to correct a false assumption that is easy to make: we are not *less blessed* than the people who witnessed them firsthand. Our vision of God is not compromised because approximately thirty-five hundred years have elapsed since these events or because they come to us in a book instead of firsthand seeing and hearing. In fact—and this may surprise some readers—we have something better than having been there: we have the Pentateuch.[1] We have the books of Genesis, Exodus, Leviticus, Numbers, and Deuteronomy. What I am suggesting is this: the leather-bound Bible on our nightstand, the Bible app on our phone, or the inexpensive newsprint Bible we read over lunch at the office is *even better than having been there*. Having the Bible is better than being a firsthand eyewitness to the events recorded in the Bible. Being an eyewitness to these events would have been incredible, but if we had to choose, it would be better to have the Bible than an eyewitness experience. Why? Although the Bible is historically accurate and beautifully written, it is first and foremost the precious word of God. Let's unpack that a little more.

Evangelical Christians rightly value the Bible as historically accurate. For this reason, scholars have served Christians well by painting a picture of life in the ancient world.[2] Archaeologists have excavated the ruins of ancient cities and given us a better sense

---

1   See John H. Sailhamer, *The Pentateuch as Narrative: A Biblical-Theological Commentary*, Library of Biblical Interpretation (Grand Rapids, MI: Zondervan, 1992), 445.
2   For a helpful resource in this regard, see, for example, *ESV Archaeology Study Bible*, ed. John D. Currid and David Chapman (Wheaton, IL: Crossway, 2018).

of the world that Abraham, Isaac, and Jacob inhabited. Ancient scrolls—not just of biblical texts, but from Israel's neighbors—have given us a better picture of the belief system of the Egyptians and the Canaanites, the Amalekites and the Jebusites, and many other ancient peoples. Since the Bible is historically accurate, a study of the history of Israel and her neighbors can provide insights on the biblical text. *The Bible is history.*

Evangelical Christians also rightly value the Bible as well-written literature. Since the biblical books were written and assembled with care, the way the material is presented is worth studying. For this reason, scholars have served Christians well as they have described the literary forms of the biblical books.[3] Studies of characterization and literary conventions have provided great insights into the biblical stories. *The Bible is literature.*

Evangelical Christians also rightly value the Bible as the precious word of God. Although human authors were used, and although their personalities, writing styles, and research are evident in the biblical books, the Bible is "living and active" and "breathed out by God" (2 Tim. 3:16; Heb. 4:12). This means that the Bible is the God-inspired *interpretation* of the events that it records. As such, the Bible is the revelation of what God was doing in the midst of these historical events. The Bible focuses our attention on God—who he is and how he relates to his creation. More than merely recording what happened in history, and more than merely giving us a beautiful piece of literature, the Bible reveals God. It is theology. *The Bible is the precious word of God.*

This also means that the Bible is selective in what it records and focused on its primary objective: to make people "wise for

---

3 For a helpful resource in this regard, see, for example, *ESV Literary Study Bible*, ed. Leland Ryken and Philip Graham Ryken (Wheaton, IL: Crossway, 2020).

salvation" (2 Tim. 3:15). As a selectively written book, it does not tell us everything about everything, nor does it intend to: "The secret things belong to the LORD our God, but the things that are revealed belong to us and to our children forever, that we may do all the words of this law" (Deut. 29:29). The Bible *does not* tell us whether snakes had legs before the fall into sin or what Moses had for breakfast before he confronted Pharaoh. This means that it will leave many questions unanswered. But the Bible is the precious revelation about the most important answers to life's most important questions. In particular, the Bible reveals God in a way that will lead us to an eternal, glorious, all-satisfying relationship with him.

Do you see why we can claim that we have something better than having been there? In the Pentateuch we have the Holy Spirit–inspired, living and active, God-breathed interpretation of the events as they occurred in history, with a focus on who God is and how we can be in right relationship with him. In these important ways, we have something that the firsthand eyewitnesses did *not* have!

The Pentateuch Is the Book of Moses

Since the Pentateuch is a precious treasure, what can we learn about its human author and its makeup? At this stage we can notice what the Bible itself asserts: Moses wrote the Pentateuch, and he wrote a unified book.

Moses Was the Greatest Old Testament Prophet

In the context of the horrible slavery of God's people, in Exodus 2 we meet a baby named Moses. Although Egypt's leader had ordered the Israelite children to be thrown into the Nile River to drown, Moses's mother placed him in a waterworthy basket of reeds and set him off on the water. Although every mother would be horrified by this scene, the Hebrew word used for that little basket is significant: it was a *teva*. *Teva* is a Hebrew word used to describe only two things in the entire Old Testament, and both of them were seaworthy vessels. The first was Noah's ark, and the second was this basket made for baby Moses.

While this is not plain when we read the Bible in English translations, for the first (Hebrew) readers of the book of Exodus, this word link would have been noticeable and clear. It would have served as a signal that Moses was going to be special. Just as YHWH had raised up and protected Noah from the raging waters by means of an ark, could it be that YHWH was about to do the same with this baby named Moses? The miraculous rescue of Moses by Pharaoh's daughter and the irony that Moses's mom was paid to nurse him only confirm our suspicions: he was going to be special. In fact, readers who know the end of the story will spot another irony: the one who would ultimately conquer Pharaoh and Egypt was earlier rescued from infanticide by the daughter of Pharaoh. So for the first forty years of Moses's life, he was raised in the house of Pharaoh, with all of its benefits. These would have included an elite education, which would have equipped Moses for a writing project he would take up many years later—the Pentateuch![4]

The rest of Moses's life can be summarized more briefly. When he was forty he murdered an Egyptian man whose body he hid in the sand. When he was confronted about this by an Israelite, he realized that he would be found out, so he was forced to flee for his life. As D. L. Moody put it, "Moses spent forty years thinking he was somebody; forty years learning he was nobody; and

4 As Stephen put it in Acts 7:22, "Moses was instructed in all the wisdom of the Egyptians."

forty years discovering what God can do with a nobody."[5] Over this second set of forty years—of learning in the wilderness that he was a nobody—Moses married a priest's daughter, had children, encountered YHWH in the burning bush, received a call by YHWH to go back to Egypt in order to bring Israel out, obeyed that call, confronted Pharaoh with ten plagues, and led Israel out of Egypt. Then over the third set of forty years, Moses received the instruction (Hebrew, *torah*) of YHWH on Mount Sinai, oversaw the construction of a tent in which YHWH would dwell among his people, frequently met with YHWH in this "tent of meeting," led a stubborn people, prepared those people to enter the promised land after a forty-year hiatus in the wilderness, wrote the Pentateuch, and died on a mountain in view of (but outside) the promised land.

After recording Moses's death, the book of Deuteronomy concludes with three verses of reflection (as you read this quote, remember that this English translation supplies the title "the LORD" for the Hebrew name YHWH):[6]

There has not arisen a prophet since in Israel like Moses, whom the LORD knew face to face, none like him for all the signs and the wonders that the LORD sent him to do in the land of Egypt, to Pharaoh and to all his servants and to all his land, and for all the mighty power and all the great deeds of terror that Moses did in the sight of all Israel. (Deut. 34:10–12)

This was a look back from some distance. Along with the account of Moses's death earlier in the same chapter, this material was added under the inspiration of the Holy Spirit by an unnamed author. And

5 D. L. Moody, cited at Quotefancy, accessed January 29, 2021, https://quotefancy.com/.
6 See this book's preface for a more thorough explanation.

the point is this: none of the other Old Testament prophets had measured up to Moses. YHWH knew Moses face-to-face. Moses accomplished greater signs and wonders and mighty power and great deeds. If the bulk of the Pentateuch was written by Moses—excluding, for example, his death notice and this word about his superiority as a prophet—this means we should read it with great interest. Not only is the Pentateuch the product of a great man of God; it is also the product of *Moses*, the greatest prophet in the entire Old Testament.

Moses Was Author of This Book

J. R. R. Tolkien's *The Lord of the Rings* is my favorite work of fiction. As we examine its contents, we can notice that it is one book and three books and six books all at the same time. Are you confused yet? *The Fellowship of the Rings* includes books 1 and 2 of the larger story, and it was first published in 1954. *The Two Towers* followed later the same year, making up books 3 and 4 of the larger story. Finally, *The Return of the King* was released in 1955, and it concluded the series with books 5 and 6. *The Lord of the Rings* is six books. It is three books. And it is one book. Each of the six books forms an essential part of the story, but each also relates to the one coherent larger story.

Even those who are casually familiar with the Bible may be aware that it identifies Moses as the author of its first five books. For example, Jesus referred to "Moses and all the Prophets" (Luke 24:27; cf. 16:31). To understand what he meant, we need to recognize that the Hebrew Old Testament has a different order of books from our English translations. In line with our English translations, the first section of the Hebrew Old Testament is made up of the first five books—what Jews call "the *Torah*," and what most Christians call "the Pentateuch." Unlike our English translations, the second section of the Hebrew Old Testament is called "the Prophets," and is made up of Joshua, Judges, Samuel, Kings, Isaiah, Jeremiah, Ezekiel, and the Twelve (Minor Prophets). This means that when Jesus referred to "Moses and the Prophets," he was speaking about the first two-thirds of the Old Testament. For our purposes, we can notice that Jesus was claiming Moses as the author of the Bible's first five books.

There is another important way the rest of the Bible refers to the Pentateuch. On the one hand, these books are "Moses," or "*Torah*," but on the other hand, I invite you to read the following passages and see if you can spot another, related title:

And they set the priests in their divisions and the Levites in their divisions, for the service of God at Jerusalem, as it is written in the Book of Moses. (Ezra 6:18)

On that day they read from the Book of Moses in the hearing of the people. And in it was found written that no Ammonite or Moabite should ever enter the assembly of God. (Neh. 13:1)

But he did not put their children to death, according to what is written in the Law, in the Book of Moses, where the LORD commanded, "Fathers shall not die because of their children, nor children die because of their fathers, but each one shall die for his own sin." (2 Chron. 25:4)

And they set aside the burnt offerings that they might distribute them according to the groupings of the fathers' houses of the lay people, to offer to the LORD, as it is written in the Book of Moses. And so they did with the bulls. (2 Chron. 35:12)

And as for the dead being raised, have you not read in the book of Moses, in the passage about the bush, how God spoke to him, saying, "I am the God of Abraham, and the God of Isaac, and the God of Jacob"? (Mark 12:26)

Did you see it? In each case, the Bible—including Jesus in the Gospel of Mark—refers to the Pentateuch as "the Book of Moses." And did you notice that the word "Book" is singular? There is a very real sense that the Pentateuch consists of five distinct books with their own unique features. But there is also a sense in which the Pentateuch is a *book*, a coherent work with a single storyline.[7]

Think of the way the story of Genesis ends where the book of Exodus picks up, and also the way the larger storyline and themes of each book build on the developing narrative. The Pentateuch is

---

7   See Sailhamer, *Pentateuch as Narrative*, 1. We should add that just as Luke wrote an orderly narrative about Jesus after much research—especially speaking to eyewitnesses (Luke 1:1–4)—so Moses employed research in writing the Pentateuch. For example, Num. 21:14 refers to "the Book of the Wars of the LORD" as a record of Israel's military history. Also, since Moses was not alive during the events recorded in the book of Genesis, he would have employed written and orally transmitted research for the writing of this entire book. Next, since other sections of the Pentateuch record long speeches by Moses, we are not told whether he wrote those speeches out or was helped in this task by a scribe. For example, the book of Deuteronomy is largely made up of three long speeches by Moses. Finally, we have already noticed that the end of Deuteronomy records the death of Moses and a reflection on his superiority as a prophet. This suggests that God inspired a later author (or authors) to make these types of small additions in order to bring the work to completion. For helpful resources that speak to these types of issues, see especially Jason S. DeRouchie, "Deuteronomy," in *What the Old Testament Authors Really Cared About: A Survey of Jesus' Bible*, ed. Jason S. DeRouchie (Grand Rapids, MI: Kregel Academic, 2013), 140; Daniel I. Block, *Covenant: The Framework of God's Grand Plan of Redemption* (Grand Rapids, MI: Baker Academic, 2021), 8.

"the book of Moses." Like *The Lord of the Rings*, it is meant to be read as a coherent whole.

As our book on the Pentateuch unfolds, we are going to practice this as we read each part in relation to the larger story. Just to whet our appetite, think for a moment about creation. Although debates about Genesis 1 and 2 abound, John Sailhamer has cautioned that instead of first asking "How do these chapters relate to the theory of evolution?" we should *primarily* ask, "What is the significance of these chapters as the introduction to the Pentateuch?"[8] This is a different question than most people bring to these chapters, but it is the most important question we can ask if we are going to interpret them as they were meant to be read—in relation to the rest of the story.[9] We will have to wait until chapter 1 of this book to unpack Sailhamer's answer, but for now we can conclude that since the Pentateuch is meant to be approached as a book, each part should be read in light of the whole.

The Pentateuch Is the Book of Redemption

We have seen that the Pentateuch is the precious word of God, written by the greatest prophet in the entire Old Testament, and that it is made up of five books with one unified story. We have also noticed that the bulk of the biblical story—from Genesis 3:15 to the end of Revelation—is a record of God's work of redemption. Since the Pentateuch is the first act in this epic of redemption, and since each of our nine chapters will focus on a theme from the Pentateuch in

8   See Sailhamer, *Pentateuch as Narrative*, 81.

9   I am not denying the importance of also thinking through the creation account in relation to contemporary theories of world origins. In fact, I teach an upper-level Hebrew course in which we spend a great deal of time discussing this very issue. In my introductory Bible courses, however, I spend my class time asking and answering this primary question of how Genesis 1–2 should be read as the introduction to the Pentateuch.

relation to this larger story, it is important that we understand what the word *redemption* means. For some readers, *redemption* may seem vaguely familiar but difficult to define with precision. For others, it may look like a fancy word that is completely unfamiliar. If we lived in Bible times, however, everyone would have understood this word because it was commonly used in regular life.

In the ancient world, redemption was not associated first with religion. In the context of the ordinary, *redemption* referred to "the rescue of an individual from a difficult obligation by means of a monetary payment."[10] It should not surprise us that ours is not the only age in which people sometimes "get in over their heads" and can't make payments they had committed to or uphold their end of an obligation they had promised to carry out. In the twenty-first-century Western world, this can result in a bank foreclosing on a person's mortgage or even jail time for a person who fails to follow through on an obligation. In the ancient world, getting in this bind could have resulted in various outcomes, including the loss of property or indentured servitude (i.e., an agreement that binds one person to be the servant of another). And the only hope for such an impoverished person was redemption.

To avoid getting bogged down by listing every situation in which this word could be used, we name just a few here. In the Old Testament we find examples of the closest family member stepping in to redeem a person in desperate circumstances (e.g., Ruth 3:12–13). We see the redemption of land and houses (e.g., Lev. 25:25), the redemption of people whose financial obligations led them to sell themselves into indentured servitude (e.g., Lev. 25:47–55), and the redemption of a wife whose husband had died

---

10 Jeremiah Unterman, "Redemption: Old Testament," in *Anchor Yale Bible Dictionary* (New York: Doubleday, 1992), 5:650.

and left her without the means of supporting herself financially (e.g., Deut. 25:5–10, Ruth).[11]

If the everyday meaning of *redemption* in the ancient world involved the rescue of a person out of a situation over which they were powerless, it is fitting that the biblical authors also used this word to describe the way God works for his people. And the exodus from Egypt is the favored Old Testament paradigm for this type of redemption. Since we are going to spend an entire chapter on this awesome event, for now we can simply observe that in the book of Exodus, God redeemed Israel from their slavery in Egypt in order to make them his special people (see Ex. 6:6–7). The entire nation of God's people were helpless slaves, and YHWH came to redeem them out of slavery and to himself—it was a physical *and* a spiritual rescue. Then in the New Testament, the word *redemption* is used to describe God's work of delivering his people from spiritual bondage and to himself. This was accomplished by the death and resurrection of the Lord Jesus.[12]

The everyday meaning of *redemption* in the ancient world involved the rescue of the desperate. In the Old Testament this type of redemption was the responsibility of one's closest relative. Therefore, it makes wonderful sense that the biblical authors presented God's work of salvation from Genesis to Revelation as *a grand story of redemption*. Sandra L. Richter has put it beautifully:

> Can you hear the metaphor of Scripture? Yahweh is presenting himself as the patriarch of the clan who has announced his intent to redeem his lost family members. Not only has

---

11 This is not an exhaustive list of examples. For such a study that is geared more toward academic readers, see Unterman, "Redemption: Old Testament," 5:650–54.

12 See Gary S. Shogren, "Redemption: New Testament," *Anchor Yale Bible Dictionary*, 5:654.

he agreed to pay whatever ransom is required, but he has sent the most cherished member of his household to accomplish his intent—his firstborn son. And not only is the firstborn coming to seek and save the lost, but he is coming to share his inheritance with these who have squandered everything they have been given. His goal? To restore the lost family members to the [house of their father] so that where he is, they may be also. This is why we speak of each other as *brother* and *sister*, why we know God as *Father*, why we call ourselves *the household of faith*.[13]

All of a sudden, *redemption* is an understandable word. And in the context of the biblical story, it is also a wonderful word.

The Path Ahead

The larger plot line of the Bible is a story of redemption. Since the Pentateuch is the most foundational portion of the Bible, understanding the dawning of redemption in this section will equip us to understand all of Scripture. Therefore, the goal of this book is to trace nine major themes about redemption through the Pentateuch in order to equip readers with a "road map" to navigate the details. We will begin with creation as the theater of redemption before considering the promise of redemption as it was given in the garden of Eden. We will also notice the lineage of redemption in the genealogies and the guarantee of redemption in the covenants. After surveying redemption accomplished in the exodus event, we will shift gears and notice some themes that relate to those YHWH

13 Sandra L. Richter, *The Epic of Eden: A Christian Entry into the Old Testament* (Downers Grove, IL: IVP Academic, 2008), 45. For Richter's helpful and readable study of redemption in the context of the ancient world and the Bible, see 21–46.

had redeemed. While the *torah* (or instruction) taught God's people how to live as the redeemed, the tabernacle, priesthood, and sacrifices were provisions for the redeemed. Finally, we will notice that unbelief resulted in a delay for the redeemed, and blessings and curses functioned to warn the redeemed.

Looking Forward to Christ: A Prophet Like Moses

The subtitle of this book relates the story of the Pentateuch to "the hope of the gospel." This reflects the way each chapter will conclude, by looking forward to Christ. Since the Bible narrates a grand story of redemption, and since the gospel of Jesus Christ is the ultimate fulfillment of the hope set forth in the Old Testament, each chapter will model a look forward in the timeline of the biblical story to its New Testament fulfillment. In keeping with the goal of this book, instead of providing all the answers, these sections will be designed to model connections and to equip readers to make other connections on their own.

Earlier in this introduction, we noticed that Moses was the greatest prophet in the entire Old Testament (see Deut. 34:10–12). Why? Because YHWH knew him face to face. And Moses also accomplished greater signs and wonders and mightier power and greater deeds than any other Old Testament prophet. However, there is a promise from earlier in Deuteronomy that instructs us to read these last three verses of the book with a sense of anticipation: "I will raise up for them a prophet like you [Moses] from among their brothers. And I will put my words in his mouth, and he shall speak to them all that I command him" (Deut. 18:18). If the Pentateuch concludes with a reflection that no prophet like Moses had arisen since, this verse in the middle of Deuteronomy tells us that we should expect this kind of awesome prophet to come. This is one of many ways the entire Old Testament builds up tension, because prophet after prophet arose and many of them were incredible, but none of them was like Moses.

Then in the New Testament we meet Jesus, who taught with authority (Matt. 7:29) and was identified as a great prophet living among the people (Luke 7:16). On the road to Emmaus he was identified further as "a prophet mighty in deed and word before God and all the people" (Luke 24:19). Philip said of Jesus that he was "him of whom Moses in the Law and also the prophets wrote" (John 1:45), and when the people saw the feeding of the five thousand they exclaimed, "This is indeed the Prophet who is to come into the world" (John 6:14; cf. 7:40). Throughout the New Testament Jesus is identified as the long-expected prophet like Moses! In fact, according to the book of Hebrews he is *better* than Moses: "For Jesus has been counted worthy of more glory than Moses. . . . Now Moses was faithful in all God's house as a servant, to testify to the things that were to be spoken later, but Christ is faithful over God's house as a son" (Heb. 3:3, 5–6). Praise God that this ultimate prophet has come, who is himself the Word of God (John 1:1).

Discussion Questions

1. As you read some of the challenges in applying the Pentateuch to life in the twenty-first century, which ones resonated most with you? Can you think of others that are also a challenge?

2. Survey your group: have you ever heard it suggested that from Genesis 3:15 to the end of Revelation, the Bible narrates the story of God's redemption of a people for himself?

3. The author argued that in the Pentateuch we have something even better than being a firsthand witness. As you consider his reasoning, do you agree or disagree? Give reasons for your answer.

4. Other than *Pentateuch*, what are some biblical options of a name for this portion of Scripture? Why do these names help us to approach these books in an understanding way?

5. In the ancient world, what was the everyday meaning of the word *redemption*? Discuss the way the biblical authors applied this same word to God's work of salvation for his people.

6. As we "look forward to Christ," we find that he is the long-awaited prophet like Moses who was to come into the world. In addition to the examples provided in this chapter, can you think of any other New Testament passages that speak about Jesus this way?

1

Creation

The Theater of Redemption

I CAN VIVIDLY REMEMBER THE SCENE: one night at our family supper table during fourth grade, my parents asked me what I was learning in school. I replied that the earth is billions of years old, plants and animals evolved gradually over that time, and humans are descended from monkeys. This was completely new information to me, and I thought they would be proud that I was listening during class. Instead, my parents told me that they did not agree with my teacher. This amounted to a mini crisis in my nine-year-old world. My teacher was one of the best in the school. As a strict authoritarian, she commanded respect, and she was a pleasure to learn from. For the first time in my life, I had learned about the theory of evolution, and since that day I have been conscious of living in a society that holds this as the dominant view of world origins.

Apart from those raised outside of the Western public school system, many readers of this book will relate to my story. We should never underestimate the impact of teaching evolution in public schools. Among its many effects, having this theory presented as fact by a respected authority figure to young and impressionable students has meant that Western readers approach the first chapters of Genesis with different questions and a different set of lenses from those who lived during the previous few thousand years. Although today's readers tend to primarily relate the creation account of Genesis 1 to the theory of evolution—whether "making Genesis fit" with evolution or using Genesis to disprove it—in this chapter we will learn a different, more foundational question that arises from our approach to the Pentateuch as the book of Moses.

Although asking how Genesis 1 relates to the theory of evolution is important in light of the dominant worldview in the West,[1] this is not the *first* question the Bible leads us to ask. With John Sailhamer we should first ask why a well-structured Pentateuch—the book of Moses—begins with the creation account?[2] In this chapter we will seek to hear Genesis 1 through the ears of its first readers, and in light of this most foundational question. We will be led to stand in awe of our Creator, and we will be given iron for our spiritual bones that cannot come from merely viewing Genesis 1 as grounds for debate. As we gain this foundational understanding of Genesis 1, we will be equipped to answer the question about why this chapter was placed first in the Pentateuch. Finally, we will look forward, from Genesis 1 to Christ, before we conclude with some questions to help readers think through the teaching a bit more.

---

1   Particularly helpful in thinking through the various views on these issues is Matthew Barrett and Ardel B. Caneday, eds., *Four Views on the Historical Adam*, Counterpoints, ed. Stanley N. Gundry (Grand Rapids, MI: Zondervan, 2013).

2   See John H. Sailhamer, *The Pentateuch as Narrative: A Biblical-Theological Commentary*, Library of Biblical Interpretation (Grand Rapids, MI: Zondervan, 1992), 81.

Understanding Genesis 1

It would be a shame to encounter Genesis 1 and never stand in awe of God. According to this passage, he is the God who speaks, and creation obeys. He is the God who forms and fills and orders and graciously gifts. Perhaps the best way to grasp the chapter as a whole is by thinking about the background information, the primary story, and the climax.

The Background Information

This may sound obvious to some, but we should not forget that the first readers of Genesis were native Hebrew speakers. This means that certain insights that come from educated Bible teachers today would have been plain and intuitive to the first readers of Genesis. We can imagine the wilderness wanderers—from the period of the book of Numbers—as they heard Aaron read his brother's fresh manuscript of Genesis for the first time. In the way the first few lines were constructed in Hebrew, it would have been clear to these readers (or more properly, hearers) that they were getting essential background information before the main focus of the story was told. There are technical terms for this that seminary students can learn in their second-year Hebrew classes, but for now let's notice that the first two verses of Genesis 1 are not the main focus of the chapter. The main focus of the chapter is the days of creation— Genesis 1:3–2:3. In Hebrew, Genesis 1:1–2 provides the essential *background information* that will equip us as readers to understand the main point of the story.[3] Far from being unimportant, this

---

3 In biblical Hebrew, the main focal story is driven by a verb form called either *wayyiqtol* or "imperfect with the waw consecutive." Put simply, we can think of a string of verbs, each of which is preceded by the conjunction *and*. When there is a long string of these verb forms in Hebrew, readers know that the main point of the story is being told. Sequences of these

information is essential. It was written to give us a sense of the larger scene before the more particular focus of the chapter unfolds.

The first verse opens the Pentateuch: "In the beginning, God created the heavens and the earth" (Gen. 1:1). In seven words (in Hebrew), we learn that God existed in the beginning, and that he created everything—the mention of "the heavens and the earth" is a Hebrew way of saying, "these two things and everything in between." Next, in verse 2, we find that creation was not yet complete: "The earth was without form and void, and darkness was over the face of the deep." However, a "without form and void" (or "formless and empty") creation was not left on its own, because "the Spirit of God was hovering over the face of the waters" (1:2). The image is of a mother bird incubating her nest, only here the Spirit of God was incubating the unformed and empty creation.[4] With a building sense of anticipation, we can expect that something good was about to happen.

The Primary Story

Genesis 1:3 begins a series of verb forms in Hebrew that tell us that the main point of the story is beginning, and these continue all the way to Genesis 2:3. This means that the days of creation is the primary story that Genesis 1 was written to convey. We'll see that on the first three days God created the environment, and on the next three days God created the creatures to inhabit that environment.

Perhaps the first thing we are meant to notice about these days of creation is the majesty of God. When we read, "And God said,

---

verb forms are broken for various reasons: to give background information that is essential for understanding the main story (e.g., Gen. 1:1–2), or to report direct speech when people in the story are quoted, for example.

4 The only other passage that employs the Hebrew verb translated as "hovering" in Gen. 1:2, is Deut. 32:11–12, where the ESV translates it as "flutters."

'Let there be light,' and there was light" (1:3), we encounter a God who spoke creation into existence. When we read, "God saw that the light was good" (1:4), we encounter a God whose creation was a good thing. When we read, "God called the light Day, and the darkness he called Night" (1:5), we encounter a God who named the good thing he had just spoken into existence. And when we read, "And there was evening and there was morning, the first day" (1:5), we encounter a God who accomplished these things in a single day.[5] Our Creator is awesome!

The next thing we notice about these days of creation is their incredible symmetry. We have witnessed the Spirit of God incubating unformed and empty creation in Genesis 1:2. Now, the focus of the six days of creation is on forming the formless and filling the emptiness:

A. Forming the Formless: Days 1–3a
    Day 1: light
    Day 2: sky/expanse
    Day 3a: dry land and seas
B. Filling the Emptiness: Days 3b–6
    Day 3b: seed-bearing vegetation
    Day 4: sun, moon, and stars

---

5 While some readers may immediately be tempted to relate this to the theory of evolution, I suggest that restraint is in order as we seek to encounter this text through the eyes and ears of its first readers and hearers. However this issue is ultimately solved, at this point we can notice with Andrew Steinmann that the text simply presents the six days of creation without qualification. He adds, "There are compelling reasons for understanding [Gen.] 1:1–31 as depicting six actual, regular days. All six days of creation are defined as the passing of both evening and morning, and the mention of *days and years* on the fourth day (v. 14) refers to normal days and years." Andrew E. Steinmann, *Genesis*, Tyndale Old Testament Commentaries (Downers Grove, IL: IVP Academic, 2019), 61; emphasis original. For a helpful and brief discussion of why he believes this, see 59–62.

Day 5: living creatures in water, birds in heavens

Day 6: animals fill the earth; humanity rules the earth

So we see that on the first three days God created the environment, and on the next three days God created the creatures to inhabit that environment.

Still more symmetry is discovered when we zoom in on the general pattern in each act of creation: (1) God commanded: "Let there be"; (2) creation obeyed: "and there was"; (3) God surveyed: "And God saw that it was good" (4); God named: "God called" (5); "And there was evening and there was morning, the __ day." As this occurs over and over through Genesis 1, we gain a sense that God is an orderly Creator.

Finally, God rested on the seventh day, not because he was tired, and not because he would now be uninvolved with the world, but because his work of creation was complete.[6] There was no more creating work to do.

The Climax

If the focus of Genesis 1 is on the days of creation, the climax of the days of creation is found on the second half of day six—the creation of humanity in the image and likeness of God. This event as the climax of creation is made clear as we notice its details. First, as the following chart by Peter Gentry illustrates, the creation of humanity takes up much more space than the rest:[7]

---

6 Although a more thorough discussion of God's rest on the seventh day is beyond the scope of this book, interested readers should see especially L. Michael Morales, *Who Shall Ascend the Mountain of the Lord? A Biblical Theology of the Book of Leviticus*, New Studies in Biblical Theology 37, ed. D. A. Carson (Downers Grove, IL: InterVarsity Press, 2015), 45–48.

7 Excerpted from Peter J. Gentry and Stephen J. Wellum, *Kingdom through Covenant: A Biblical-Theological Understanding of the Covenants*, 2nd ed. (Wheaton, IL: Crossway, 2018), 218. Used by permission.

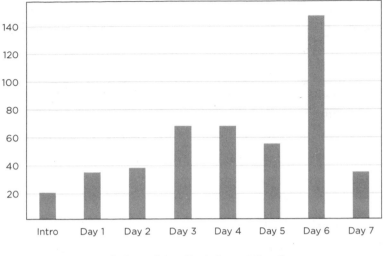

Words Describing Each Day of Creation

So there are more words used to describe the creation of humanity than any other aspect of creation.

Next, not only are more words used to describe day six, but the kinds of words that are used are different from the other days. We have already noticed the incredible symmetry in the days of creation, but on the second half of day six God broke the rhythm. Over and over again in our story, we read the words "Let there be" (1:3, 6, 14), or, "Let the earth sprout" (1:11), or similar phrases. But in 1:26, the phrase shifts to "Let us make." This phrase seems to hint at plurality of persons within the Godhead. It also seems to communicate a more intimate involvement of the Creator in this act of creation.

The words "in our image" and "after our likeness" are also used to describe the creation of humanity. God is spirit and cannot be represented by any image (Ex. 20:4; John 4:24). And all of creation is his handiwork (cf. Gen. 1:1–2:3). According to this passage, humanity in his image and likeness would be more like God than any other aspect of creation, and humans would image forth the invisible Creator to the rest of creation. Stephen G. Dempster explains further:

> If the terms "image" and "likeness" stress the unique relationship humanity has to its Creator, they also indicate the exalted, regal role humanity plays in its natural environment. The male and female as king and queen of creation are to exercise rule over their dominion, the extent of which is the entire earth.[8]

As the passage continues, we find just that: humanity ruling over creation as God's vice-regents (1:26). And later, in 1:28, this ruling over creation is expressed in filling the earth with other image bearers as well as in subduing creation. As God's vice-regents, royal humanity was called to steward creation.

The summary statement in 1:27 is essential for understanding the importance of *both* men *and* women in God's creation. It is less common today to use words such as *man* or *mankind* for groups of men and women. Instead, we tend to use *people* or *humanity* as a way of communicating more precisely about groups of mixed gender. In biblical Hebrew, however, terms like *man* or *mankind* can be used to refer to mixed groups of people, or they can also be used to refer to gender-specific groups of men. The context in which these words are used will ultimately determine their meaning. This is why the specificity of the language in Genesis 1:27 is so important: "So God created man in his own image, in the image of God he created him; male and female he created them." This verse

---

8 Stephen G. Dempster, *Dominion and Dynasty: A Theology of the Hebrew Bible*, New Studies in Biblical Theology 15, ed. D. A. Carson (Downers Grove, IL: InterVarsity Press, 2003), 59.

is a summary statement about God's creation of man in his image. But the third clause adds "male and female he created them." In other words, in case there was any question whether only men were created in the image of God—misinterpreting "man" in Genesis 1 as gender-specific—the language of the third line clarifies this. The author was clear that both men and women were created equally in the image of God.

If we live in the West, teaching about the equality of men and women most likely resonates as a given that our culture affirms. But through the eyes of its first readers, this would have been radical and countercultural teaching. The first readers of Genesis lived in a patriarchal society in which men were viewed as more important than women, and in which women were not highly valued. In the face of this came the Bible's radical teaching that both men and women are equally valuable before God.

According to Genesis 1—where more words are used to describe the creation of humanity than any other aspect of creation, where God was more intimately involved in this act of creation than any other, and where the job of ruling over creation was given to people, and not animals—humanity made in the image and likeness of God was (and is) the most important aspect of creation. In fact, we can think of every other aspect of creation as *preparatory* for the creation of humanity as the crowning climax. This is why the chapter concludes with a "very good" evaluation by God (1:31). Now that his image bearers had been created, the world was complete.

The supreme importance of humanity over the rest of creation is also displayed by the relationship between Genesis 1 and 2. Although we will spend our entire next chapter walking through the story of the garden of Eden, we should notice first that Genesis 1–2 tells the story of creation *twice*. Peter Gentry explains:

The approach in ancient Hebrew literature is to take up a topic and develop it from a particular perspective and then to stop and take up the same theme again from another point of view. This pattern is recursive in order to present full-orbed ideas. . . . When one discourse is heard against the background of another, together they function like the left and right speakers of a stereo, and we have an idea that is like Dolby surround sound or a holographic image.[9]

To switch analogies, Genesis 1:1–2:3 tells a "zoomed-out camera lens" story of creation—it gives us the big picture. And Genesis 2:4–25 tells a "zoomed-in camera lens" story of creation—it gives us more intimate details that focus on the creation of the man and the woman. When read together, they give us two perspectives on the one act of creation. Back to Gentry's analogy, they tell the story of creation in Dolby surround sound (or even Dolby Atmos!).

Peter Gentry's insight also tells us something about the importance of humanity: the story of their creation was so monumental that it warranted a Dolby surround-sound moment. Humanity was the only aspect of creation made in the image and likeness of God and called to rule over creation, and whose creation story was told in Dolby surround sound, with two complementary chapters in a row. Although we could say a whole lot more about the teaching in Genesis 1, we now have a handle on its most significant features.

The Main Point of Creation

Now that we understand the main focus of Genesis 1, we can return to our question: Why does the Pentateuch—the book of

---

9   Gentry and Wellum, *Kingdom through Covenant*, 489–90.

Moses—begin with the story of creation? First, remembering the identity and life situation of the Pentateuch's first readers helps with some insights. Let's recall that the first readers of Genesis were the wilderness generation—the people who had grown up as slaves in Egypt. In that Egyptian context, idolatry abounded. Among those idols, the sun god was Re, the Nile River was venerated as the source of life, and Pharaoh was worshiped as a god. In the face of this, Genesis 1 made a startling claim: the God of this nation of former slaves created the sun, gathered the waters into oceans and rivers, and created all people in his image and after his likeness. Not only did this make Pharaoh a creature under Israel's God; it also put him on a level footing with Israel—the nation of slaves. In the face of this idolatrous Egyptian culture, all people—whether Jew or non-Jew, male or female, slave or free—were created in the image and likeness of God. They were all equally image bearers, they were all equally not gods, and they were all equally more like God than any other aspect of creation. In fact, they were all equally vice-regents under God who were to rule and subdue creation. In the context of the Pentateuch and its first readers, the God who appeared to his people in the midst of their idolatrous context in Egypt is the God of creation. He is over all the so-called gods of Egypt because he created all things.[10]

Next, let's remember what the first readers of Genesis had just experienced: the exodus from Egypt. And what led to this exodus? The ten plagues. In the context of Genesis 1, as YHWH brought Egypt to its knees by turning the Nile River into blood, killing all of the livestock, and sending all the other plagues leading up to the death of the firstborn son, he was temporarily returning Egypt to

---

10 Other biblical passages teach that God made all things out of nothing. Interested readers can look up Isa. 45:7–18; Rom. 11:36; Col. 1:16–17; Heb. 1:2–3; Rev. 4:11.

precreation chaos. For a brief time, Egypt—the greatest superpower nation of the day—was, at least in part, "formless and empty" (Gen. 1:2). This nation that thought its pantheon of gods was great and its power unshakable, found out that it was dependent on the God of its nation of slaves for its every breath. As Pharaoh wept at the bedside of his dead firstborn son, he was learning the painful lesson that this child—who would have become the next Pharaoh and, therefore, worshiped as a god—had died at the command of the Creator of all. L. Michael Morales continues the story to the Red Sea crossing, observing that "Egypt is steadily de-created until Pharaoh's hosts are submerged in the waters of chaos, whereas Israel emerges from those waters re-created."[11] When its first readers (or hearers) encountered the book of Genesis, they learned the wonderful lesson that their deliverance from Egypt was not accidental; the very first words of Genesis led them to see that their deliverer was also the Creator of all.

This leads to the most important answer to our question, Why was Genesis 1 placed as the first chapter of the Pentateuch? Yes, it showed that Israel's God was supreme over the so-called gods of Egypt and all other nations. Yes, it explained that the plagues on Egypt amounted to a temporary and piecemeal return to precreation chaos, as YHWH showed his power to the nation oppressing his people. But more than these things, Genesis 1 had a very positive effect on God's people. In the Pentateuch we encounter a God who called a people to himself, who made promises, and who sealed those promises with covenants. When its first readers encountered the Pentateuch, they did so as the objects of God's mercy and favor. They were the ones who had received glorious

11 Morales, *Who Shall Ascend the Mountain of the Lord?*, 78.

promises. And they were the ones in covenant relationship with YHWH. In this context, we can see that the God of the great and mighty covenant promises is also the God of *creation*. He is good, and he is God over all. Nothing in the cosmos can stop him from being faithful to his promises, because nothing in the cosmos is outside of his control. He is not a localized deity. Since the God of the covenants is the God of creation, all of creation is the theater of redemption, and this God's promise is sure.[12]

Looking Forward to Christ: "In the Beginning Was the Word"

John's Gospel begins with the phrase, "In the beginning was the Word" (John 1:1). This is a clear and deliberate echo of the first verse of the Pentateuch, Genesis 1:1. And in that Old Testament passage, how did God create? Through speaking, through his *word*. Throughout the Old Testament, God's word also accomplished deliverance for his people (e.g., Ps. 107:20) and revealed truth to his people (e.g., Jer. 1:4).[13] Although space restrictions do not allow us to survey everything the word of God accomplished throughout the Old Testament, we can notice that this first line of John's Gospel primarily points back to the creation account.

As the first chapter of John's Gospel continues, however, we see that the Word he wrote about was a *person*. In John 1:1–18, the Word was in the beginning, he was with God, and he *was God* (1:1). All things were made through him (1:4), and he was the true light who gave those who received him, who believed in his name, the right to become children of God, to be born of God (1:9, 12–13). As John's prologue continues, "The Word became

12 See Sailhamer, *Pentateuch as Narrative*, xix, 81.
13 For these and other examples, see D. A. Carson, *The Gospel according to John*, Pillar New Testament Commentary, ed. D. A. Carson (Grand Rapids, MI: Eerdmans, 1991), 115.

flesh and dwelt among us, and we have seen his glory, glory as of the only Son from the Father, full of grace and truth" (1:14). D. A. Carson explains: "In short, God's 'Word' in the Old Testament is his powerful self-expression in creation, revelation and salvation, and the personification of that 'Word' makes it suitable for John to apply it as a title to God's ultimate self-disclosure, the person of his own Son."[14] Jesus is the Word.

What does this mean for our reading of Genesis 1? In the very least it means that God the Son, the second person of the Trinity, was intimately involved in creation. As the Word, he was the agent of creation—all things were made through him (John 1:3), or as the apostle Paul put it, "by him all things were created" (Col. 1:16). Jesus is God. He is the preexistent one who was there at creation, and he is the Word through whom the world was created. In this way, the New Testament brings clarity on something that was not yet fully revealed in the Old Testament: all three persons of the Trinity were intimately involved in creation. For this reason, a Christian reading of Genesis 1 will have two levels. First, we must discipline ourselves to read it in its context in the Pentateuch and hear its message through the ears of its first hearers: the God of the covenants is the God of creation. And, second, we must read it with the insight that our Savior, who died on the cross for our sins, is the one through whom the world was created.

Before we conclude this chapter, we will revel in one more incredible Christian truth. The apostle Paul wrote to the Corinthian church: "Therefore, if anyone is in Christ, he is a new creation. The old has passed away; behold, the new has come" (2 Cor. 5:17). Do you see what this means? It means that when you and I turned

14 Carson, *Gospel according to John*, 116.

from our sins and trusted Christ, nothing less than a work of new creation happened in us. The same God who brought the cosmos into existence in Genesis 1 spoke with exactly the same creative power in our hearts. When a person becomes a Christian, he or she becomes a new creation.

Discussion Questions

1. When did you first encounter the theory of evolution? Tell the story to your group.

2. Why is it so important to ask why Genesis 1 was placed as the first chapter of the Pentateuch?

3. Share one of this chapter's insights on Genesis 1 that was new to you.

4. What is the most essential function of Genesis 1 as the first chapter of the Pentateuch?

5. Did Jesus have a role in creation?

6. Reread 2 Corinthians 5:17. In light of our fresh focus on Genesis 1, how does this truth make you feel?

2

Eden

The Promise of Redemption

IN THE EARLY 1940S, Walt Disney had an idea. In collaboration with conductor Leopold Stokowski, he would employ a breakthrough technology in his new movie, *Fantasia*. Instead of the standard mono sound of the day, he would use surround sound during the movie's "Flight of the Bumblebee" segment. By this means, Disney would immerse theatergoers into the score so that "the musical sound of the bumblebee could be heard flying all around the audience, not just in front of them."[1]

As Peter Gentry taught us in our previous chapter, the Bible opens with a surround-sound moment. While Genesis 1:1–2:3 tells the story of the days of creation, it is followed by the story of Eden in Genesis 2:4–3:24. When read together, these two complementary accounts paint a more full-orbed portrait of creation than

1 Michael Miller, "The History of Surround Sound," *InformIT*, September 24, 2004, https://www.informit.com/.

either of them could accomplish on their own. In a way, thousands of years before Walt Disney in the 1940s and the Dolby stereo of the 1970s, Moses was the ancient innovator when he employed surround sound in the first chapters of the Bible.[2]

As we look at its details, Genesis 2:4–3:24 is clearly a single story. First, its setting is the garden of Eden. Second, this portion of Scripture also employs a unique name for God. In Genesis 1:1–2:3, God is referred to as "Elohim," a Hebrew word that is roughly equivalent to our English word *God*. In a chapter that focuses on the majestic big picture of creation, *God* did the creating. In Genesis 2:4–3:24, the author switched to "YHWH Elohim" (or, "YHWH God"), and this pair of words is rarely used together in the rest of the Old Testament. In the context of the Pentateuch, the name YHWH is associated with God's personal relationship with his people, the covenant promises he made to them, and the redemption he accomplished for them—we will learn more about this in chapter 5 on the exodus. Coupled together, the title "YHWH God" emphasizes the personal nature of the majestic Creator God.

The story of Eden is absolutely essential for understanding the dawning of redemption in the Pentateuch. This story begins by presenting the template of redemption, as it paints a picture of the perfect home of the first man and woman (Gen. 2:4–25). Next, it presents the need for redemption, with the account of the fall into sin (Gen. 3:1–24). Finally, in the midst of the bleakness of sin, the main point of the story of Eden is found in the first glimmer of gospel hope in the entire Bible (Gen. 3:15). For this reason, I've

---

2 This phenomenon is witnessed throughout the Bible. In fact, the entire books of Matthew, Mark, Luke, and John create a surround-sound moment at the beginning of the New Testament, as they paint a more full-orbed portrait of Jesus than reading only one Gospel could do on its own.

titled this chapter "Eden: The Promise of Redemption." Let's take a closer look at each of these three points—the template, the need, and the promise of redemption—before we look forward to Christ from this awesome story.

The Template of Redemption (Gen. 2:4–25)

The story begins in paradise, sort of. Actually, Genesis 2:4–25 tells the story of the creation of the perfect earthly home for the man and the woman. Like the zoomed-out story of Genesis 1, everything in this portion of Scripture prepares for the crowning climax of creation: the man and the woman as God's vice-regents in a perfect world. Because the fall into sin occurs in the second half of the story of Eden (Gen. 3), we will see that Genesis 2 also provides the template for redemption's future end goal; after Genesis 3, the rest of the Bible builds toward a return to a new and better Eden.

The story begins with a heading: "These are the generations of the heavens and the earth when they were created, in the day that the Lord God made the earth and the heavens" (Gen. 2:4). As I will explain in the next chapter, Genesis includes ten headings like this one, and each is built into the story. This first heading reveals that these verses tell the story of the creation of the heavens and the earth—all things—by YHWH God.

The story continues by giving an intimate, zoomed-in portrait of the freshly created earth—plants had not yet sprung up, rain had not yet come, there were no people to work the ground, and a mist watered the whole ground (2:5–6). In this context, "the Lord God formed the man of dust from the ground and breathed into his nostrils the breath of life, and the man became a living creature" (2:7). We can see that the zoomed-in camera lens of Genesis 2 adds a lot to the story—the "Let us make man in our image" from Genesis 1 is even more intimate in Genesis 2, with YHWH God acting as a master potter who formed the man and then breathed life into his nostrils. Then in 2:8 YHWH God planted a garden in Eden and put the man there—nothing less than a lush place would do for the crowning climax of his creation.

As the story continues, YHWH God caused trees to sprout, and they were beautiful to look at and good for food (2:9). We worship an artistic and abundant God—he chose to create a beautiful world that was filled with sustenance for his image bearers. Among these were the tree of life, and the tree of the knowledge of good and evil (2:9), and we will learn more about these as the story continues. We also learn that this place of abundant beauty and sustenance was a place where life could be abundantly sustained—it was the *source* of four rivers, and these reached out into places filled with gold and jewels (2:10–14). While Eden was the most abundant place in creation, it was not the only location of abundance.

The mention of gold, bdellium, and onyx in 2:10–14 would have especially caught the eye of the first readers of Genesis, because these adorned the tabernacle of YHWH.[3] In fact, the thoughts of these readers would have been taken to the tabernacle at the very first mention of the garden, in 2:8. When most twenty-first-century Western readers think of a garden, we imagine little patches cut out of manicured lawns where flowers and shrubs are planted. But in ancient Hebrew thought, a garden was an enclosed place where high shrubs created walls around the perimeter to shelter the inside

---

3 The tabernacle was a large tent structure where YHWH dwelled and where he was worshiped. We'll explain more about this structure in later chapters.

from the elements.[4] Having an enclosed cube with gold and jewels where YHWH God could intimately live with his people sounds a whole lot like the later tabernacle—a theme we will explore more thoroughly in chapter 7.

The connection to the tabernacle is even stronger in 2:15: "The LORD God took the man and put him in the garden of Eden to work it and keep it." On the one hand, the words *work* and *keep* teach us that work and responsibility and creativity existed before the fall into sin. In Genesis 3 we are going to learn that work as sweaty toil only began after sin entered the world. Work is intrinsically good, and work is only difficult today because of the effects of sin. On the other hand, the first readers of Genesis would have noticed a clear connection between the calling of the man to "work" and "keep" the garden, and the calling of the priests to "minister" and "serve" in the tabernacle, because exactly the same Hebrew words are used. The same Hebrew word is translated "work" in Genesis 2:15 and "service" in Numbers 8:25–26; 18:5–6. And the same Hebrew word is translated "keep" in Genesis 2:15 and "keep guard" in Numbers 8:25–26; 18:5–6.[5] For the first readers of Genesis, YHWH God's commission of the man sounded as priestly as it did practical.

Finally, the first readers of Genesis would have noticed that the entrance to Eden was from the east (Gen. 3:24), "which was also the direction from which one entered the tabernacle and, later,

4 Peter Gentry adds that in the Old Testament, "walls surrounded both royal gardens (2 Kings 25:4; Neh. 3:15; Jer. 39:4; 52:7) and vineyards (Prov. 24:30–31; Isa. 5:5)." Peter J. Gentry and Stephen J. Wellum, *Kingdom through Covenant: A Biblical-Theological Understanding of the Covenants*, 2nd ed. (Wheaton, IL: Crossway, 2018), 245.

5 I first learned this insight from John H. Sailhamer, *The Pentateuch as Narrative: A Biblical-Theological Commentary*, Library of Biblical Interpretation (Grand Rapids, MI: Zondervan, 1992), 100–101.

temples of Israel, and would be the same direction from which the latter-day temple would be entered (Ezek. 40:6)."[6] While Genesis 1 paints a portrait of humanity as kingly figures who acted as God's vice-regents over creation, Genesis 2 emphasizes humanity as priestly figures who dwelled in the presence of YHWH God.

With the words "you may" and "you shall not," 2:16–17 introduces the first parameters in the garden paradise: "And the LORD God commanded the man, saying, 'You may surely eat of every tree of the garden, but of the tree of the knowledge of good and evil you shall not eat, for in the day that you eat of it you shall surely die'" (Gen. 2:16–17). Notice that this command was positive— "You may surely eat of every tree." Also notice that there was only one tree in the entire garden from which the man could not eat. Finally, notice that this command was given before the creation of the woman—this was a command that he would need to relay to his wife. This will be important to remember as we walk through Genesis 3 and the fall into sin.

In the context of a perfect creation, the assessment by YHWH God in 2:18 was jarring: "It is *not good* that the man should be alone; I will make him a helper fit for him." While each act of creation in Genesis 1 was assessed as "good," or in the case of humanity, "very good," the only "not good" thing in God's early assessment of creation was that the man was alone; creation was incomplete without the woman. According to Genesis 2:18, she would be a "helper" who, in a literal translation of the Hebrew, would be made "according to his opposite." The picture here is of a team of two equals, with the woman taking the same "helper"

6   G. K. Beale, *The Temple and the Church's Mission: A Biblical Theology of the Dwelling Place of God*, New Studies in Biblical Theology 17, ed. D. A. Carson (Downers Grove, IL: InterVarsity Press, 2004), 74.

title as YHWH himself, who is often portrayed as the helper of his people (e.g., Ex. 18:4; Deut. 33:29; Ps. 70:5 among over a dozen Old Testament references to YHWH as his people's helper).

The tension then increased as YHWH God created the animals and brought them to the man for naming—surely an act of sovereignty for his vice-regent (2:19–20). YHWH God then caused a deep sleep to fall on the man; he took one of his ribs and literally "built" the rib that he took from the man into a woman, and he brought her to the man. The man's response was telling: "At last!" So YHWH God presented the woman to the man as his wife, and we learn that in marriage "a man shall leave his father and his mother and hold fast to his wife, and they shall become one flesh" (2:24). The scene ends with the man and his wife naked but feeling no shame. With the creation of the woman and the blessing of the first marriage, the garden paradise was finally complete.

The Need for Redemption (Gen. 3:1–24)

Genesis 3 begins with a rare assessment of a biblical character's inner life. Normally in Hebrew narrative (i.e., stories), we learn a person's character through their *outward* actions—what happened—and a snapshot of their inner life is reserved for poetry (e.g., the book of Psalms; Ex. 15 within the larger story of the book). But the character of the serpent was so essential for the story that we are told he was more crafty than any other beast of the field. We have already noticed that the only prohibition in the garden paradise—not to eat of the tree of the knowledge of good and evil—was given to the man *before* the woman was created. It would have been the man's job to teach his wife this command. In Genesis 3 this crafty serpent focused his attention on the woman—the one who had received the command secondhand.

Through a series of exchanges, the serpent filled the woman's mind with half-truths—true enough to be compelling—as he tempted her to eat. The first thing we notice is the name used for God: the narrator referred to him as YHWH God throughout the story of Eden, but the serpent and the woman referred to him as "Elohim" (God). The personal, covenant name YHWH was noticeably absent from their talk.

The command from YHWH God in Genesis 2:17 had begun with words of abundance, before the man was told of the one tree from which he could not eat: "You may surely eat of every tree of the garden." But the serpent twisted this into "Did God actually say, 'You shall not eat of any tree in the garden'?" (3:1). When the woman pointed to the one tree from which they were not allowed to eat, the serpent then directly opposed the word of God with an overt lie: "You will not surely die" (3:4). And then he planted a seed of doubt in her mind: "For God knows that when you eat of it your eyes will be opened, and you will be like God, knowing good and evil" (3:5). The woman ate, and the text tells us that "she also gave some to her husband *who was with her*, and he ate" (3:6). This means that the man—who was the direct recipient of the command not to eat from that one tree—was with her all along as she was being tempted, and he remained silent. Stephen G. Dempster summarizes the gravity of this scene: "The flagrant rebellion against the divine word by the pinnacle of creation, which has just been invested with the divine rule, is a heinous crime against the cosmos and its Creator."[7]

The impact of this first sin was felt immediately. Prior to it, "the man and his wife were both naked and were not ashamed"

---

7   Stephen G. Dempster, *Dominion and Dynasty: A Theology of the Hebrew Bible*, New Studies in Biblical Theology 15, ed. D. A. Carson (Downers Grove, IL: InterVarsity Press, 2003), 66.

(2:25). Immediately after the first sin, "the eyes of both were opened, and they knew that they were naked" (3:7). So they sewed leaves together in an attempt to cover their shame. Then they heard the sound of YHWH God walking in the garden in the cool of the day—notice that hearing their God walking in their midst was a familiar sound, and also notice that the weather was pleasant. But the two sinners hid themselves among the trees of the garden. Through an exchange of calling and responding and admitting nakedness, and then admitting sin, the scene moved to blame-shifting: "The man said, 'The woman whom you gave to be with me, she gave me fruit of the tree, and I ate'" (3:12). Let the blame game begin! According to the man, their sin was the woman's fault, and it was ultimately YHWH God's fault—"you gave her to me." When YHWH God then addressed the woman, she continued the blame game: "The serpent deceived me, and I ate" (3:13).

This clear admission of guilt then led to judgment by YHWH God. The serpent was cursed above all livestock, he would crawl on his belly, and he would be at enmity with the woman (3:14–15). Sidney Greidanus notes that this is the first occurrence of a curse in the Bible. As the opposite of blessing, "God's curse removes creatures from his blessing."[8] In Genesis 1:1–2:3, God *blessed* the animals, the human beings, and the seventh day. After the fall into sin, YHWH God then *cursed* the serpent, the ground, and in the next chapter, the murderer Cain. This is the bleakest of scenes.

As the story continues, so do the punishments for sin. The woman would have pain in childbearing, and desires at odds with those of her husband. The couple would be in a battle to domineer

---

8   Sidney Greidanus, *Preaching Christ from Genesis: Foundations for Expository Sermons* (Grand Rapids, MI: Eerdmans, 2007), 80.

each other from this point forward (3:16). And in the case of the man, the ground was cursed, and he would eat of it in pain all the days of his life. This cursed ground would produce thorns and thistles, and the man would get food through sweat-filled labor until he returned to the ground—a reference to his coming death (3:17–19). The last consequence was likely the worst: the sinful man and woman could not be allowed to eat from the tree of life and live forever, so they were sent out of the garden of Eden. With a cherubim and a flaming sword guarding the way to the tree of life, the sinful man was sent out to work the ground from which he was taken; life would be a struggle until finally, the man and the woman would eventually die (3:20–24).

It is difficult to overstate the horrendous impact of this one act of disobedience—all human history has felt its repercussions. Prior to the fall into sin, there was simply no pain, no aching longing that went unmet, no disease, and no death. No one was sinned against or sinned against another. As L. Michael Morales put it:

> This fallen condition is also the genuine cause of our fears, anxieties, depression, and restlessness—we are exiles, alienated fugitives, within a cosmos that was created to be our home with God. And yet there is nothing within creation itself that can fulfill our soul's capacity and longing to have fellowship with the One who transcends the night sky and all the works of his hands.[9]

Apart from an act of amazing grace, the outlook for the man and the woman was absolutely bleak.

9 L. Michael Morales, *Exodus Old and New*, Essential Studies in Biblical Theology 2, ed. Benjamin L. Gladd (Downers Grove, IL: IVP Academic, 2020), 9.

The Promise of Redemption (Gen. 3:15, 20–21)

If Genesis 3 was entirely about sin and punishment, YHWH God would have been completely just, and we would have been completely without hope; this darkest of days would have been absolutely bleak. As the apostle Paul said about the resurrection, so we can say about the dawning of redemption in Genesis 3: if there is no gospel hope in Genesis 3, "Let us eat and drink, for tomorrow we die" (1 Cor. 15:32). But praise God that he chose to give glimmers of hope, words and actions of mercy, in the midst of this horrible scene.

The first hint of hope comes as we notice what did *not* happen: YHWH God did not obliterate the man and the woman immediately after the first sin. In fact, Genesis 5 tells us that the man (Adam) lived 130 years before he fathered Seth (his third son), and then another eight hundred years before he died at the age of 930. We know that Cain and Abel were born after Genesis 3, so we can be sure that Adam lived at least eight hundred years after the fall into sin. To be sure, the effects of death impacted Adam and Eve immediately after the first sin, as their bodies and the world around them were brutally affected. But they did not immediately die.

The next glimmer of hope came as YHWH God was cursing the serpent. In the midst of that curse, YHWH God addressed the serpent: "I will put enmity between you and the woman, and between your offspring and her offspring; he shall bruise your head, and you shall bruise his heel" (3:15). Scholars throughout church history have referred to this verse as the proto-gospel, the first gospel, because it is the first glimmer of gospel hope that set in motion the entire story of redemption that is unfolded in the rest of the Bible.

We will unpack this in more detail in the next chapter, but for now we can notice that in Genesis 3:15, two offspring are mentioned: the offspring of the serpent and the offspring of the woman. And these two offspring would be in a conflict that would end in the striking of mutually fatal blows: the offspring of the woman would bruise (or "crush") the head of the offspring of the serpent, and the offspring of the serpent would bruise (or "crush") the heel of the offspring of the woman. Therefore, this verse promises a coming death for the serpent's offspring along with the death of someone in the lineage of the woman.

From the perspective of this verse, we are given reason to hope, but that hope needs to be filled out with more explanation. And that is exactly what the rest of the Bible does—it tells the story of redemption by our God of amazing grace. From the perspective of the New Testament, we can say that as Jesus was hanging on the cross, it seemed as though Satan had the upper hand—because the Son of God was dying a real death. But by his death and resurrection, Jesus won the ultimate victory over sin, Satan, and death *for us*.

As Genesis 3 continues, more glimmers of gospel hope appear. Although pain in childbearing would be a horrible consequence of the fall into sin, this also meant that the man and the woman would be able to have children—and one of those children would win the ultimate victory over the offspring of the serpent (3:15–16). This is emphasized again in 3:20, where "the man called his wife's name Eve"—a Hebrew word that means "life"—"because she was the mother of all living."

On the surface, 3:21 may seem like no big deal. But when "the Lord God made for Adam and for his wife garments of skins and clothed them," this is in direct contrast to 3:7, where the immediate reaction to sin is reported: "Then the eyes of both were opened, and they knew that they were naked. And they sewed fig leaves together and made themselves loincloths." Sin ushered in shame, which ushered in an attempt to cover their shame. But only YHWH God could adequately accomplish this—with animal skins instead of fig leaves. This is even more powerful when we think about how animal skins are acquired: an animal must die. This is the first hint that in order for sinners to have their shame relieved, their sin needs to be covered by the death of something innocent. For the first readers of Genesis, this would have clearly called to mind the sacrificial system. For us—with the perspective of the New Testament—we can say that this scene is yet another hint at the ultimate sacrifice of Christ that would come at the climax of the biblical story.

Finally, in the horrible scene of expulsion from the garden of Eden, there was also a measure of mercy. YHWH God's purpose in driving the man and woman out was to keep them from eating of the tree of life and living forever. Sidney Greidanus explains: "Can you imagine what a disaster it would be if sinful human beings, like the ancient murderer Lamech or the modern murderer Hitler, would live forever? No matter how great the reign of terror of evil people, we know that they will all die and their evil reign will come to an end."[10] Although this is certainly not a glimmer of hope, it does provide some form of relief: as we live in a fallen world, we can remember that reigns of terror by Hitler and other tyrants will necessarily end.

Looking Forward to Christ: A Crown of Thorns and a New and Better Eden

Near the end of three of the Gospels, we encounter a scene of mockery. In Matthew, Mark, and John, Jesus had been arrested, charged, and sentenced to die on a Roman cross. The soldiers then

---

10 Greidanus, *Preaching Christ from Genesis*, 82.

took him into the governor's headquarters and gathered the whole battalion before him. They stripped him and put a scarlet robe on him. And then we read, "Twisting together a crown of thorns, they put it on his head and put a reed in his right hand. And kneeling before him, they mocked him, saying, 'Hail, King of the Jews!' And they spit on him and took the reed and struck him on the head" (Matt. 27:29–30). After this, they stripped him of the robe, put his own clothes back on him, and led him away for crucifixion.

By mocking Jesus in this way, these biblically illiterate Roman soldiers symbolized more than they could have possibly understood. In their actions, they unwittingly echoed elements from the early chapters of Genesis—this is why three of four Gospel writers draw our attention to it. We saw in our last chapter that men and women in the image and likeness of God were designated as vice-regents over the rest of creation. According to this scene, before he went to the cross, Jesus wore a crown. Although he was being mocked as a so-called king, he was, in fact, *the* King over all.

But Jesus's crown was of thorns. This hearkens our minds back to Genesis 3 and YHWH God's words to the man:

> Cursed is the ground because of you; in pain you shall eat of it all the days of your life; *thorns and thistles* it shall bring forth for you; and you shall eat the plants of the field. By the sweat of your face you shall eat bread, till you return to the ground, for out of it you were taken; for you are dust, and to dust you shall return. (Gen. 3:17–19)

Among sin's consequences was a cursed ground that produced thorns and thistles. This means that by wearing a crown of thorns, the Son of God was bearing on his very head the curse of sin for us.

He would go on to an agonizing death on a Roman cross, but the most horrifying part came when he bore the wrath of God—the ultimate curse—that our sins deserved: "And about the ninth hour Jesus cried out with a loud voice, saying, 'Eli, Eli, lema sabachthani?' that is, 'My God, my God, why have you forsaken me?'" (Matt. 27:46). By wearing a crown of thorns, King Jesus symbolized outwardly what was going on inwardly, when as the ultimate priest—better than sinful priest Adam in the garden of Eden—the sinless Son of God bore the curse of our sin before the Father.

We could write an entire book on what this awesome sacrifice purchased for us, but we will consider just one: through his death, Jesus won an eternity for his people in the new heavens and the new earth—a new and better Eden. While the first Eden was glorious but lost, the new and better Eden will be permanent and eternal. While the first Eden contained precious jewels, the new and better Eden will have walls adorned with every kind of jewel and streets of pure gold (Rev. 21:18–21). While the first Eden needed sun and moon—because the radiant presence of YHWH would be removed after the fall into sin—in the new and better Eden, there will be no need for sun or moon and there will be no night, because "the glory of God gives it light, and its lamp is the Lamb" (Rev. 21:23). While the first Eden was the template, the new and better Eden will be the substance. While the first Eden allowed for a serpent and temptation, all sin and every sinner—and even the tempter himself—will be shut out of the new and better Eden (Rev. 20:10; 21:8, 27; 22:3, 15). While the way was barred to the tree of life after the fall into sin, in the new and better Eden it will be in the middle of the city's street, and available for the healing of the nations—for all whose robes are washed in the blood of the Lamb (Rev. 22:2, 14). This is our hope!— the new heavens and the new earth will be better than the first Eden. Let's close by reveling a bit more:

> Then I saw a new heaven and a new earth, for the first heaven and the first earth had passed away, and the sea was no more. And I saw the holy city, new Jerusalem, coming down out of heaven from God, prepared as a bride adorned for her husband. And I heard a loud voice from the throne saying, "Behold, the dwelling place of God is with man. He will dwell with them, and they will be his people, and God himself will be with them as their God. He will wipe away every tear from their eyes, and death shall be no more, neither shall there be mourning, nor crying, nor pain anymore, for the former things have passed away." And he who was seated on the throne said, "Behold, I am making all things new." (Rev. 21:1–5)

What a glorious hope!

Discussion Questions

1. Why does Genesis include two accounts of creation?

2. Why is Genesis 2:4–3:24 best read as one single story?

3. How does the garden of Eden foreshadow the tabernacle?

4. In the story of the temptation, why is it significant that the serpent first twisted God's word before he directly opposed it?

5. Of the various glimmers of gospel hope after the fall into sin, which stuck out to you as particularly glorious?

6. In the New Testament description of the new heavens and the new earth, what aspects stuck out to you as particularly glorious?

7. Read Revelation 12:9 and 20:2. What do these two verses teach us about the true identity of the "ancient serpent" from Genesis 3? Next, read Revelation 20:10. What implication does this verse have for the new and better Eden that is the hope of all believers in Jesus?

3

Genealogy

The Lineage of Redemption

THE SCENE IS FAMILIAR TO MANY OF US: we wake up in the
morning with an awareness of our need for the word of God. We want
to see the world through the lens of the word, and we want to be led
into prayer by the word. We are also conscious of the limited time we
have before the demands of our day creep in, so we roll over, grab our
Bible, and open to the place we left off the day before. And we read:

> This is the book of the generations of Adam. When God created
> man, he made him in the likeness of God. Male and female he
> created them, and he blessed them and named them Man when
> they were created. When Adam had lived 130 years, he fathered
> a son in his own likeness, after his image, and named him Seth.
> The days of Adam after he fathered Seth were 800 years; and he
> had other sons and daughters. Thus all the days that Adam lived
> were 930 years, and he died. (Gen. 5:1–5)

Okay, we tell ourselves, *that first bit felt about as edifying as reading the phone book, but let's keep reading*: "When Seth had lived 105 years, he fathered Enosh. Seth lived after he fathered Enosh 807 years and had other sons and daughters. Thus all the days of Seth were 912 years, and he died" (Gen. 5:6–8). At this point we begin to panic, and our fears are confirmed as our eyes scan down the page. This is an entire chapter of genealogy, of births and deaths and really long lifespans. We had wanted the voice of Scripture to be crisp and clear, an encounter with the living God at the beginning of our day. But instead we are experiencing a muted voice that is easy to ignore.[1] As we survey the book of Genesis, we find three chapters devoted *entirely* to genealogies (Gen. 5; 10; 36). That is a lot of "phone book" reading!

In this common scene from our personal Bible reading, it is possible that our understanding of Scripture led us to anticipate an encounter with God. After all, we know that "the word of God is living and active" (Heb. 4:12). And we also know that "all Scripture is breathed out by God and profitable for teaching, for reproof, for correction, and for training in righteousness, that the man [or woman, or boy, or girl] of God may be complete, equipped for every good work" (2 Tim. 3:16–17). As our approach to every passage of Scripture is informed by the Bible's own teaching about itself, we realize that any time we fail to encounter God in the Bible, the problem is with us, not the Bible.

---

1   Although it is hard to convey in print, and although only some readers will be familiar with the illustration, I often liken the voice we instinctively hear when reading the Bible's genealogies to the voice of the teacher in the old *Peanuts* cartoons—"wa, wa, wa wa, wa wa wa." In other words, we may be aware that someone is speaking, but we have no idea what is being said because we are not paying attention.

In light of this, is there any hope that reading a biblical genealogy can lead us to encounter God? The (perhaps surprising) answer is yes, but first we need to learn about the purpose of these passages. So far in this book we have noticed that the Bible tells the grand story of redemption, and that the Pentateuch narrates the dawning of redemption. We have also seen that creation is the theater of redemption, and Eden records the first promise of redemption. In this chapter, we will see that the genealogies (or general statements of family lineage) in Genesis sketch *the lineage of redemption*. To help us get a handle on these surprisingly important passages, we are going to unpack four truths about the genealogies in Genesis before we close by looking forward to Christ in light of them:

1. Genesis 3:15 is the key to understanding the family lineage passages in the rest of the book.
2. Genesis is framed around ten statements of family lineage.
3. Each time we encounter a family lineage passage in Genesis, we need to ask an important question.
4. Understanding the family lineage passages in Genesis helps us interpret all of Genesis.

Let's dive in and learn together.

Genesis 3:15 is the Key to Understanding the Family Lineage Passages in the Rest of the Book

In the last chapter we encountered gospel hope in the bleakest of scenes. We remember that as a part of his curse on the serpent, YHWH God said: "I will put enmity between you and the woman, and between your offspring and her offspring; he shall bruise your head, and you shall bruise his heel" (Gen. 3:15). Now we can build on our learning: not only is this the first glimmer of gospel hope in the entire Bible, but in the context of this discussion of genealogies, notice that it also points to two lineages.[2]

It is understandable that the horrible scene from Genesis 3 would produce conflict between the serpent (the deceiver) and the woman (the deceived). However, YHWH God took it a step further by extending the conflict to the "offspring" (or seed) of the serpent and the "offspring" (or seed) of the woman. In other words, there will be a lineage for the serpent and a lineage for the woman, and they will be in conflict with one another. Ultimately, the offspring of the woman will "bruise" (or crush) the head of the offspring of the serpent, and the offspring of the serpent will "bruise" (or crush) the heel of the offspring of the woman. When my kids were younger, I liked to explain this verse to them by asking, "How do you kill a snake?" They would reply, "You cut off (or crush) its head." And then I would ask them, "How does a poisonous snake kill people?" And they would reply, "By biting their heel (because that is what the slithering snake can reach)." This is a hint, therefore, that the offspring of the serpent and the offspring of the woman would both die as they struck each other with mutually fatal blows.

From the perspective of the first readers of Genesis, this is a promise in need of further "filling out," and that is exactly what the rest of the Bible does. From the vantage point of a completed Bible, we can say that on the cross, Satan and his "offspring" (those opposed to YHWH and his purposes) crushed the heel of the offspring of the woman—the Lord Jesus. But because of the resurrection on the third day, the Lord Jesus crushed the head of

---

2 My thinking on this topic was born in 2008, when I read the following in preparation for a sermon series through Genesis: Bruce K. Waltke and Cathi J. Fredricks, *Genesis: A Commentary* (Grand Rapids, MI: Zondervan, 2001), 93–94.

the serpent and his offspring—he gained the final victory over sin and all its effects, *for us*! Genesis 3:15 is certainly the first glimmer of gospel hope in the entire Bible, a passage that could only be fully understood in hindsight, when the events to which it points had taken place.

Now that we understand Genesis 3:15, we can turn back to the book of Genesis and notice that the verse begins to get "filled out" in this fifty-chapter book. As the first glimmer of gospel hope, Genesis 3:15 teaches us that when we read through Genesis, we ought to be looking for the offspring of the serpent and the offspring of the woman. Now we can see how statements of family lineage in Genesis may be significant! Before we explain this further, it is important to understand the structure of Genesis.

Genesis Is Framed around Ten Statements of Family Lineage

In our Bibles, chapters and verses are helpful. Can you imagine a pastor telling his congregation to open their Bibles to the sixteenth page, the second column, the third paragraph, and the fourth line? It would be impossible to get everyone on the same page. But chapters and verses were not a part of the original Bible manuscripts. They were added later as a helpful way of "getting on the same page," but they were not inspired. As we approach the book of Genesis, we find that its original author (Moses) framed it around two halves and ten sections. This *is* a part of the original shape of the book.

As we look at the big picture of Genesis, we find that its first "half" is found in Genesis 1:1–11:26. These chapters record what biblical scholars refer to as "primordial history." The term *primordial* refers to the beginning of time, so *primordial history* refers to all of history from creation to the fall to the flood to the Tower of Babel.

As we read the long genealogies in Genesis 5 and 10, we find that many generations of people lived during this time in world history.[3]

In the big picture of Genesis, we find that its second "half" is found in Genesis 11:27–50:26. These chapters record what biblical scholars refer to as "patriarchal history." If a *patriarch* is the male head of a family or tribe, *patriarchal history* in these chapters of Genesis concerns the four generations from Abraham (the patriarch) to Isaac to Jacob to the twelve sons of Jacob. In this second half of Genesis, we encounter only four generations in thirty-nine chapters. So Genesis is split into two uneven "halves": primordial (ancient) history (Gen. 1:1–11:26) and patriarchal history (Gen. 11:27–50:26).

Genesis is also split into ten sections, and this is something we will spot only if we are using a literal translation of the Bible. As Moses was shaping this book of beginnings, he used the phrase "These are the generations" to structure his material. In the big picture of Genesis, this phrase is used to introduce ten different sections in the book. Just as the two halves of Genesis are uneven in length, so are the ten "These are the generations" sections.

The symmetry of the book—two halves, ten sections—is even more clear when we learn that the first half of Genesis has five "These are the generations" sections, and the second half of Genesis also has five "These are the generations" sections.

Family Lineage Statements in Genesis 1:1–11:26

1. "These are the generations of the heavens and the earth when they were created, in the day that the LORD God made the earth and the heavens" (Gen. 2:4).

---

3 This is amplified even more when we consider the possibility of gaps in the genealogies. In light of Hebrew thought, it is entirely possible that "father of" sometimes meant "ancestor of" in these genealogies.

2. "This is the book of the generations of Adam. When God created man, he made him in the likeness of God" (Gen. 5:1).

3. "These are the generations of Noah. Noah was a righteous man, blameless in his generation. Noah walked with God" (Gen. 6:9).

4. "These are the generations of the sons of Noah, Shem, Ham, and Japheth. Sons were born to them after the flood" (Gen. 10:1).

5. "These are the generations of Shem. When Shem was 100 years old, he fathered Arpachshad two years after the flood" (Gen. 11:10).

Family Lineage Statements in Genesis 11:27–50:26

6. "Now these are the generations of Terah. Terah fathered Abram, Nahor, and Haran; and Haran fathered Lot" (Gen. 11:27).

7. "These are the generations of Ishmael, Abraham's son, whom Hagar the Egyptian, Sarah's servant, bore to Abraham" (Gen. 25:12).

8. "These are the generations of Isaac, Abraham's son: Abraham fathered Isaac" (Gen. 25:19).

9a. "These are the generations of Esau (that is, Edom)" (Gen. 36:1).

9b. "These are the generations of Esau the father of the Edomites in the hill country of Seir" (Gen. 36:9).

10. "These are the generations of Jacob. Joseph, being seventeen years old, was pasturing the flock with his brothers. He was a boy with the sons of Bilhah and Zilpah, his father's wives. And Joseph brought a bad report of them to their father" (Gen. 37:2).

The symmetry of Genesis is unmistakable.

Since we now understand that Genesis is structured around the phrase "These are the generations," or what we are calling "family lineage statements," we can notice a few more of their features that will equip us to see their practical significance. First, notice that these statements provide structure for the book of Genesis, with a preface and then ten sections:

Preface: Genesis 1:1–2:3
1. Genesis 2:4–4:26: The generations of the heavens and the earth
2. Genesis 5:1–6:8: The book of the generations of Adam
3. Genesis 6:9–9:29: The generations of Noah
4. Genesis 10:1–11:9: The generations of the sons of Noah: Shem, Ham, and Japheth
5. Genesis 11:10–26: The generations of Shem
6. Genesis 11:27–25:11: The generations of Terah
7. Genesis 25:12–18: The generations of Ishmael
8. Genesis 25:19–35:29: The generations of Isaac
9. Genesis 36:1–37:1: The generations of Esau/Edom (36:1, 9)
10. Genesis 37:2–50:26: The generations of Jacob

Perhaps we can think of these as the ten original (usually long) chapters in the book of Genesis.

Next, notice that five of the family lineage statements introduce a long genealogy. In each of these we find the details of the family lineage of Adam (Gen. 5:1–6:8), the sons of Noah (Gen. 10:1–11:9), Shem (Gen. 11:10–26), Ishmael (Gen. 25:12–18), and Esau/Edom (Gen. 36:1–37:1). Also, four of the ten family lineage statements introduce a story-form account of a prominent person in Genesis: Noah (Gen. 6:9–9:29), Terah (Gen. 11:27–25:11), Isaac (Gen. 25:19–35:29), and Jacob (Gen. 37:2–50:26). Other than the Noah section, the entire content of each focuses on the *children* of the person listed in the "These are the generations" saying. For example, the family lineage of Terah tells the story of Abram/Abraham. Finally, the first of the ten family lineage statements does not list a person at all: "These are the generations of the heavens and the earth" (Gen. 2:4). This creates a preface for the book of Genesis (Gen. 1:1–2:3) and an introductory section that details the early years, including creation (Gen. 2:4–4:26).

Each Time We Encounter a Family Lineage Passage in Genesis, We Need to Ask an Important Question

Now that we understand the way Genesis is structured around two unequal halves and ten statements of family lineage, we can begin to see their significance. Each time we encounter a statement of family lineage in Genesis, we must remember that we are entering a new section of the book. But Genesis 3:15 also prompts us to read each section with an important question in mind: *Will the people in this section carry on the family lineage of the woman that will lead to the ultimate deliverer who will decisively defeat the serpent and all the effects of sin?*

As we examine the material, sometimes our answer will be no; a reading of the Ishmael and Esau sections leads to this conclusion. But most of the time, these statements of family lineage either detail the family tree of or tell the story of the family line that stretches from "the woman" (Gen. 3:15) to Noah (Gen. 6:9–9:29) to Shem (Gen. 11:10–26) to Terah (Gen. 11:27–25:11, with a focus on Abram/Abraham) to Isaac (Gen. 25:19–35:29, with a focus on Jacob/Israel) to Jacob (Gen. 37:2–50:26, with a focus on his twelve sons, who would become the twelve tribes that made up the Old Testament people of God).

In other words, as we read the family lineage passages in Genesis through the lens of the promise in Genesis 3:15, we are led to the heroes of the story—the ones through whom YHWH would accomplish his promised redemption. Or, as we put it in the title of this chapter, genealogies in Genesis detail the lineage of redemption, the family line that helps to unfold YHWH's grand plan of salvation, a plan that stretches from Genesis 3:15 to the end of the book of Revelation. As we read the accounts of these "heroes," we quickly find that there was nothing in them that made them worthy of such a role in YHWH's plan—whether it was Noah sinning after the flood, or Abraham and Isaac's failures of faith, or Jacob's serial deception. This leads us to conclude that the real hero of the story—the only true hero, in fact—is YHWH God.

Understanding the Family Lineage Passages in Genesis Helps Us to Interpret All of Genesis

At this point it will be helpful—and very practical—to focus on one example of how the family lineage statements impact our interpretation and application of a passage in Genesis. Genesis 37–50 is a beloved section of the Bible, usually for its portrayal of the innocent suffering and ultimate exaltation of Joseph. Tim Rice and Andrew Lloyd Webber's musical adaptation of these chapters in *Joseph and the Amazing Technicolor Dreamcoat* is perhaps the most famous, but even those who are new to the Bible tend to be drawn to this well-told and inspiring story. As we examine the story, however, some of its chapters do not seem to fit. In particular, between the selling of Joseph into slavery (Gen. 37), and the account of Joseph in Potiphar's house (Gen. 39), we encounter a seemingly out-of-place chapter about Judah's sin with his daughter-in-law, Tamar. More than one Bible study leader or pastor has been tripped up by this chapter; how can it fit into their otherwise inspiring series through "the Joseph narrative"? As they encounter Genesis 38, they are left with a dilemma: if they skip over it, they are implicitly telling their people that it is not important, but if they dive into it, they are not sure how it relates to the overall story of Joseph (Gen. 37–50).

As we step back and read Genesis 37–50 through the lens of the statements of family lineage, the surprising insight is this: it is *not* the Joseph narrative after all! We recall that Genesis 37:2–50:26 records "the generations of *Jacob*" (Gen. 37:2). We also recall that the narrative that follows statements like this one usually details the life (or lives) of the son(s) of the person named at the section's beginning. This section is no different: Genesis 37:2–50:26 records the story of the twelve sons of Jacob. We also remember that when we interpret these fourteen chapters as "the generations of Jacob," we are meant to be asking an important question: Which character in the drama will carry on the lineage of redemption, the one who will be set apart as the human "hero" in the lineage of the woman? (Gen. 3:15).

When we interpret Genesis 37:2–50:26 through this lens, it transforms our reading. Instead of thinking of these chapters as "the Joseph narrative," we begin to see that Joseph—though very prominent in this section—would win the Oscar for *best supporting actor* in this drama of redemption. As we read to the end of the section, we find that *Judah* is the brother who will be centered out by Jacob: "The scepter shall not depart from Judah, nor the ruler's staff from between his feet, until tribute comes to him; and to him shall be the obedience of the peoples" (Gen. 49:10). Just like we can never watch a suspenseful movie in the same way twice, as we go back and reread Genesis 37:2–50:26 in light of its ending, the entire story makes much more sense.

As we read these chapters with our attention fixed on Judah, we encounter a horrible beginning, a radical transformation, and a firm resolve. Prior to this section of Genesis, we met Judah at his birth in Genesis 29:35 and found that his name means "one who is praised." Then in Genesis 35:23 we learned that he was one of six sons born to Jacob's wife Leah. Now in our current section of Genesis, we find that it was Judah who spoke up in response to the brothers' idea of killing Joseph and said, "What profit is it if we kill our brother and conceal his blood?" (Gen. 37:26). Evidently, Judah was the kind of brother who looked for profit in place of bloodguilt. In response to Judah, the brothers made a profit on Joseph and still got rid of him.

In Genesis 38 Judah was the kind of man to marry a wicked Canaanite woman—the careful reader will remember the "cursed be Canaan" passage from Genesis 9:25. Judah was also the kind of guy who would let a double widow wait in false hope that she would one day marry his remaining son. He was also the kind of man who would visit a prostitute, and who would—despite his own sexual sin—call for the burning alive of his pregnant daughter-in-law because of her sexual sin. It is not until the end of Genesis 38 that we encounter anything positive about Judah, when he exclaimed, "She is more righteous than I" (Gen. 38:26).

In the flow of the story, this will prove to be the turning point for Judah. In Genesis 43 it was Judah who spoke up and gave his father assurance that Benjamin would come back safely, or he (Judah) would bear the blame forever (v. 9). Then when the silver cup was found in the bag of Benjamin, Judah spoke up to the Egyptian official—whom he did not know was his brother

Joseph—to plead for the life of his brother Benjamin. This is the longest speech in all of Genesis, and it includes the phrase, "God has found out the guilt of your servants" (44:16). Evidently, the sin of selling Joseph still weighed on Judah and his brothers. But in this speech, Judah offered himself as a slave in place of Benjamin. Finally, in Genesis 49:10, when Jacob blessed the twelve brothers, he exalted Judah above all the others as the one in whose lineage a king would reign.

In light of this, Genesis 38—the story of Judah and Tamar—is not an out-of-place chapter in an otherwise coherent Joseph narrative. Instead, it is a pivotal chapter in the family lineage of Jacob (Gen. 37:2–50:26), in which the descendant of the woman was brought to a place of humility and transformation. This also transforms the way we read the word of encouragement in Genesis 50:20, where Joseph exclaimed to his brothers: "As for you, you meant evil against me, but God meant it for good, to bring it about that many people should be kept alive, as they are today." More than simply a general statement of general good that came from his suffering, in the flow of Genesis we can see this as a clear exclamation that *the lineage of the woman had been preserved through the trials of Joseph.* The next time we wake up in the morning and encounter a genealogy in our Bible reading, it will likely still be a bit boring to read through all the names. But now we will have a sense of why the genealogy is there and how we can properly interpret and apply it.

Looking Forward to Christ: The Family Lineage of Jesus

As we look beyond Genesis, we find that there are several other records of family lineage in the Old Testament. For example, at the end of Ruth we encounter the genealogy of King David through the lineage of Judah's sons (Ruth 4:18–22). Evidently, the promise that "the scepter/ruler's staff will not depart from Judah" (Gen. 49:10) was being fulfilled in King David. Although our English Bibles place Chronicles in the middle of the Old Testament—immediately after the books of Samuel and Kings[4]—the Hebrew Old Testament places Chronicles at the very end. Whereas our English Bibles implicitly suggest that Chronicles represents a repackaging and building on the material recorded in Samuel/Kings, the Hebrew Old Testament places it last, as a way of looking ahead with hope.

As we read Chronicles from this perspective, we find that the Hebrew Old Testament ends in a similar way as it began, with a genealogy-heavy book—this time with a book that begins with nine entire chapters of genealogy. As the author of Chronicles was beginning his work, he traced the lineage of his readers all the way back to Adam and Eve, through the offspring of the woman. The message was clear to them as they waited for full restoration after the Babylonian exile: "You can and should have the audacity to place all of your hope in YHWH's faithful restoration (see Deut. 30:1–10), because you are the very people he has promised to restore (see Gen. 3:15)." So the Old Testament is bookended with genealogy-heavy books, and these books take their interpretive cues from Genesis 3:15.

As we move to the New Testament, we discover that it begins with—you guessed it—a genealogy. This means that the Old Testament (in its Hebrew order) is bookended with genealogy-heavy

---

4 I am using "Samuel" as a short form for the books of 1 and 2 Samuel, "Kings" as a short form for the books of 1 and 2 Kings, and "Chronicles" as a short form for the books of 1 and 2 Chronicles. It is likely that each was originally divided in two because of scroll length; scribes could not fit all of the material onto a single scroll, so they needed to split each of them into two parts.

books, and the New Testament begins with a genealogy. Specifically, the Gospel of Matthew opens with these words: "The book of the genealogy [Greek: *genesis*] of Jesus Christ, the son of David, the son of Abraham" (Matt. 1:1). In other words, Matthew begins with a genealogy that stretches back to David, what is more, to Abraham. These are two key people with whom YHWH had made covenants in the Old Testament, and these covenants pointed forward in their fulfillment to Jesus. But there is a word in Matthew 1:1 that hints toward something more. When we compare its wording to the ten statements of family lineage in Genesis, we find that it matches one of them: "This is *the book* of the generations of Adam" (Gen. 5:1). No other statement of family lineage in Genesis is referred to as a "book" of the generations.

Although twenty-first-century Western Christians may be tempted to question whether this is a legitimate connection that was intended by Matthew, we need to remember that the Old Testament was not foreign territory to the authors of the New Testament; it was home turf. These people soaked in its words like many Christians today memorize the exact phrasing of Romans or Galatians. To summarize, in Matthew 1 the author traces the lineage of Jesus back to David, through Judah and Tamar, all the way back to Abraham. And his wording also echoes "the book of the generations of Adam" from Genesis 5:1. This means that Matthew was also implicitly tying the genealogy of Jesus all the way back to Adam. In other words, Jesus is set forth as a new and better Adam in Matthew's Gospel—the offspring of the woman who succeeded where the first Adam had failed.

Next, not only did Matthew begin his Gospel with a genealogy, but he frequently used Greek words that mean "to bear," or "to beget," or "to give birth," or "lineage," throughout his first two chapters. The links to Jesus as the ultimate offspring of the woman seem very clear—Jesus is the one in whom the promise of Genesis 3:15 finds its ultimate fulfillment. This is also highlighted when Matthew reveals that the one to be born to Mary is from the Holy Spirit (Matt. 1:20), that he will save his people from their sins (1:21), and that he is Immanuel—God with us (1:23, citing Isa. 7:14). Jesus is clearly the ultimate offspring of the woman, the promised Savior to come.

So far in this chapter, we have noticed that the promise of a coming offspring of the woman from Genesis 3:15 can be traced through the family lineage statements in Genesis to the family lineage passage at the end of Ruth, through the nine chapters of family lineage that begin 1 Chronicles, all the way to Jesus in Matthew 1–2. But what about the offspring of the serpent from Genesis 3:15? Does the Bible provide any clarity about the identity of this lineage? As we approach the Gospel of Matthew, we find that Jesus was opposed first by Herod. Then at the beginning of Matthew 3, people were streaming to John the Baptist in the wilderness to be baptized by him in the Jordan River. When the Pharisees and Sadducees also came out, John said to them, "You brood of vipers! Who warned you to flee from the wrath to come?" (3:7). The Greek word for "brood" comes from the same word family as "genealogy" in Matthew 1:1, and "to bear" throughout Matthew 1–2. And this word for "brood" means "offspring." In this passage, John the Baptist was calling the Pharisees and Sadducees the offspring of vipers—poisonous snakes! The kind of snakes that could bite a heel and bring death.

In this context, John the Baptist was clearly exclaiming that these Jewish religious leaders represented the offspring of the serpent from Genesis 3:15, who would bite the heel of the offspring of the woman and bring about his death. This suggests that from the outset of Matthew's Gospel, the cross was on the horizon. This also suggests that the identity of the offspring of the serpent in the Bible is anyone actively opposed to God and his people, who tried to stop God's plan of redemption. Ultimately, it was Satan himself—the one who would enter the heart of Judas, inducing him to betray Jesus to death (Luke 22:3).

In summary, the way the New Testament begins hearkens our minds back to the original gospel promise in the Old Testament—Genesis 3:15—and the way the four Gospels unfold shows the ultimate fulfillment of this promise. Praise God that as his Son was receiving the fatal snake bite on his heel, he was also dealing the fatal blow to the head of the offspring of the serpent. As he died on the cross, Jesus won the decisive victory over sin and all of its effects, and he did this *for us*. Then when he rose from the dead on the third day, he showed himself as the first fruit of this victory.

Discussion Questions

1. How do you typically respond when you come across a genealogy in your Bible reading?

2. The author argued that Genesis 3:15 is the key to understanding the family lineage statements in the book of Genesis. Restate his argument in your own words and share whether you agree or disagree. Give reasons for your answer.

3. Explain the author's argument for two uneven "halves" and ten uneven "chapters" in the book of Genesis. Have you heard this teaching before, or is this a new insight?

4. Is Genesis 38 an out-of-place chapter in an otherwise coherent Joseph narrative, or is there a better explanation for its appearance and placement in the book of Genesis?

5. In your own words, explain the link between Genesis 3:15, the Old Testament genealogies, Matthew 1–3, and the cross of Jesus.

4

Covenant

The Guarantee of Redemption

IT WAS A BEAUTIFUL DAY near the end of June, but not even bad weather could have dampened my spirits. It was my wedding day. I stood at the front of the church and looked out at family and friends. The music changed, and the congregation stood and turned to the back of the church, where my beautiful bride was entering on her father's arm. They proceeded to the front—toward me!—and hugged. Before I knew it, Natalie was on *my* arm and her dad was sitting down. On that day we sang songs of worship, listened to readings and a sermon, and continued in the formal parts of the ceremony. As we exchanged vows, Natalie and I became husband and wife. We vowed to love and cherish each other until death parts us. No matter what life would bring—better or worse, riches or poverty, sickness or health—we would be united as husband and wife. As our pastor had taught us in premarriage counseling, in that ceremony Natalie and I solemnly entered into a covenant relationship with each other.

So far in this book, we have noticed that the larger story of the Bible is a story of *redemption*, and that the first five books of the Old Testament tell the story of *the dawning of redemption*. We have also noticed that in this story of redemption, God made *promises* as he revealed more and more about his plan of redemption. In this chapter we are going to dive deeply into another glorious word related to God's work of salvation: *covenant*.

As we study the Old Testament, we discover that the Hebrew word for *covenant* occurs 287 times, and that the majority of these are between human parties. For example, we find the covenant of marriage (Ezek. 16:8; Mal. 2:14). We also find treaties between people, sometimes with the stronger party setting the terms of peace (e.g., Ex. 23:32), sometimes with the weaker party seeking terms of peace (e.g., 1 Kings 20:34), and sometimes with two equals seeking peace with one another (e.g., Gen. 21).[1] In every case, a covenant between people was a solemn and formal agreement, and it defined the terms of their relationship. George E. Mendenhall and Gary A. Herion helpfully define *covenant* as "an agreement enacted between two parties in which one or both make promises under oath to perform or refrain from certain actions stipulated in advance."[2]

Earlier in this book we noticed that the word *redemption* was commonly used in people's interactions with one another and also used to describe God's work for his people. In a similar way,

---

1 For a comprehensive analysis of the concept of covenant in the Old Testament, see Peter J. Gentry and Stephen J. Wellum, *Kingdom through Covenant: A Biblical-Theological Understanding of the Covenants*, 2nd ed. (Wheaton, IL: Crossway, 2018), 161–77, 841–904. In fact, Gentry and Wellum's entire book has had a particular shaping influence on my understanding of the biblical covenants, and therefore, the material in this chapter.

2 George E. Mendenhall and Gary A. Herion, "Covenant," *Anchor Yale Bible Dictionary* (New York: Doubleday, 1992), 1:1175.

covenants were something that people entered into with one another, and God also used this incredible word to describe the formal commitment he made to redeem his people. However, when God made covenants with his people, he was the ultimate stronger party—the Creator—who rightly set all the terms. Daniel I. Block explains:

> God the divine Suzerain initiates the covenant; God chooses the covenant partner; God declares the terms; God determines the consequences for the subjects, depending on their responses to him and his revealed will . . . and God identifies the sign of the covenant. . . . YHWH's covenant partners are never in a position to negotiate either the terms of the contract or the consequences for fidelity or infidelity; their only option is to accept or reject the relationship.[3]

In light of God's absolute power and control, it is a testimony to his awesome character that he was also so gracious. In fact, and in line with the language we have been using to frame this book, we can say that YHWH's covenants with his people represent his *guarantee* of their redemption.

While the larger story of the Bible is indeed a story of God's redemption, the six covenants between YHWH and his people are high points in the larger story. They drive the story of redemption forward because they formalize YHWH's commitment, detail his terms, and guarantee a glorious outcome.[4] As Sandra L. Richter put

---

3 Daniel I. Block, *Covenant: The Framework of God's Grand Plan of Redemption* (Grand Rapids, MI: Baker Academic, 2021), 2. The term *suzerain* will be further explained on pp. 135–36, 190–91.

4 As Stephen Wellum put it, "Progressive covenantalism argues that the Bible presents a *plurality* of covenants that *progressively* reveal our triune God's *one* redemptive plan for his *one*

it, "The Bible teaches us that redemptive history did not happen in one fell swoop. Rather, God has been leading humanity back to Eden by means of a sequence of steps, a series of rescues, a series of covenants."[5] Therefore, if we are going to understand the larger story of the Pentateuch (and the entire Bible), we will need to understand YHWH's covenants with his people. Perhaps the best way to do this is to zoom in on one of them, then zoom out to get a big-picture sense of the others, before we close by looking forward to Christ.

Zooming In: YHWH's Covenant with Abraham

The story of Abraham's life is told in Genesis 11:27–25:10. As we read these chapters, we find no less than four passages that are essential to our theme of covenants: Abram's call (Gen. 12:1–9), the cutting of the covenant (Gen. 15), the establishing of the covenant (Gen. 17), and the sworn oath (Gen. 22). As we understand these passages and their relationship to one another, we will be equipped to understand YHWH's other covenants as well.

YHWH Calls Abram

Just as most twenty-first-century marriages in the West begin long after a dating relationship has been established between the bride and the groom, so YHWH's covenant with Abram came *after* he had first initiated a relationship with him. In Genesis 12:1–3 YHWH broke into the life of Abram and called him:

---

people, which reaches its fulfillment and terminus in Christ and the new covenant." Gentry and Wellum, *Kingdom through Covenant*, 35; emphasis original.

5   Sandra L. Richter, *The Epic of Eden: A Christian Entry into the Old Testament* (Downers Grove, IL: IVP Academic, 2008), 130.

Go from your country and your kindred and your father's house to the land that I will show you. And I will make of you a great nation, and I will bless you and make your name great, so that you will be a blessing. I will bless those who bless you, and him who dishonors you I will curse, and in you all the families of the earth shall be blessed.

At first glance this passage contains one command and numerous promises, but Peter Gentry observes that the phrase translated "so that you will be a blessing" at the end of 12:2 is actually a command in Hebrew. Therefore, it would be better translated as, "Be a blessing!"[6] In light of this insight, we can notice that this call contains two commands, and each command is followed by three promises:

Commands	Promises
Go from your country and your kindred and your father's house to the land that I will show you	I will make of you a great nation
	I will bless you
	(I will) make your name great
Be a blessing	I will bless those who bless you
	him who dishonors you I will curse
	in you all the families of the earth shall be blessed

6 For a full explanation, including the technicalities of Hebrew translation, see Gentry and Wellum, *Kingdom through Covenant*, 266–79.

In the first command, YHWH called Abram to leave everything behind, and the promises associated with this command were all directed toward Abram: YHWH would make of him a great nation (despite his barren wife), YHWH would bless him, and YHWH would make his name great. Next, the second command focused on Abram's dealings with the surrounding nations: "Be a blessing!" And the promises associated with this command were all focused on what would come to those other nations as a result: YHWH would bless those who bless Abram, YHWH would curse those who dishonor Abram, and in Abram all the families of the earth would be blessed.

These commands and promises were monumental. To this point in the Bible, the focus had been on broad world history. But at this point, the rest of the story of Genesis slows down and zooms in on this one man (Abram), his son (Isaac), his grandsons (Jacob and Esau), and his great-grandsons (the twelve sons of Jacob). This was the beginning of the Jewish people—with "Father Abraham" as their head. But from the beginning, from the very first call of Abram, notice that YHWH had his eyes on bringing blessings to all the nations. This is even more shocking when we realize what had just happened in the story of Genesis: the Tower of Babel and the cursing and dispersing of the nations. In Genesis 12:1–3 YHWH revealed more about his plan to crush the head of the serpent: he would do it by getting specific, with this one man and his family, and he would do it globally, by using this family to ultimately bring blessing—to borrow a phrase from the book of Revelation—to people "from every nation, from all tribes and peoples and languages" (Rev. 7:9). In the face of Babel's judgment (Gen. 11:1–9), there was now hope of *global* redemption for all nations!

In response to this call, Abram obeyed. At seventy-five years old, he left everything behind and traveled to the land YHWH showed him. And as he traveled, he claimed the land for YHWH by building altars to him at his various stops (Gen. 12:7–8). The Canaanites had been living in the land, but with his actions Abram showed by faith that it would one day be the place inhabited by his descendants, YHWH's special people.

YHWH Cuts a Covenant with Abram

Fast-forward in our story to Genesis 15. By this time Abram's entourage was growing (to 318 men, along with their families [14:14]), and his wealth was growing (13:2). This means he was already experiencing the beginnings of the promised blessings from YHWH (see 12:2).

In this context, "the word of the LORD came to Abram in a vision: 'Fear not, Abram, I am your shield; your reward shall be very great'" (15:1). Abram responded with a question about offspring: How could YHWH fulfill his promise of making Abram into a great nation, when Abram's wife, Sarai, was barren? YHWH then assured Abram that his very own son would be his heir (15:4). This assurance was accompanied by a promise: "He brought him outside and said, 'Look toward heaven, and number the stars, if you are able to number them.' Then he said to him, 'So shall your offspring be'" (15:5). Abram then believed YHWH, and this trust that YHWH would keep his word was credited to him as righteousness (15:6).

YHWH then focused in on the land: "And he said to him, 'I am the LORD who brought you out from Ur of the Chaldeans to give you this land to possess'" (15:7). Abram then questioned how he would know he would possess this land, and YHWH commanded him to bring animals: "a heifer three years old, a female goat three years old, a ram three years old, a turtledove, and a young pigeon" (15:9). Abram's actions revealed that he knew why YHWH wanted these animals: "He brought him all these, cut them in half, and laid each half over against the other. But he did not cut the birds in half" (15:10).

Abram then fell into a very special kind of deep sleep. With only seven occurrences in the entire Old Testament, the Hebrew word translated "deep sleep" in this verse is not very common, and it is the same word used in Genesis 2:21 for the deep sleep that fell on the man so that YHWH could remove a rib and build the woman. William C. Williams adds that in the Old Testament, "Yahweh causes a deep sleep to fall on people to allow him to do his work without interference (Gen 2:21; 1 Sam 26:12; Isa 29:10) or reveal himself in a special way (Gen 15:12; Job 4:13; 33:15; Dan 8:18; 10:9)."[7] In this case, YHWH was clearly doing the latter—causing a deep sleep to fall on Abram so he could reveal himself in a special way.

In the midst of Abram's slumber, YHWH revealed something about the future: he predicted four hundred years of slavery for Abram's descendants and then a radical escape that would result from YHWH's miraculous intervention. In short, he was predicting the exodus from Egypt four hundred years before it happened. And as our scene continues, we learn: "On that day the LORD made a covenant with Abram" (Gen. 15:18).

We learn a lot about covenants from this awesome scene. First, covenants in the ancient world were made by the shedding of blood. In fact, the word translated "*made* a covenant" in Genesis 15:18 could more literally be translated "*cut* a covenant." Some might ask why a committee of professional Bible translators

---

7   William C. Williams, "רָדַם," *New International Dictionary of Old Testament Theology and Exegesis*, ed. Willem VanGemeren (Grand Rapids, MI: Zondervan, 1997), 3:1054.

would tweak the translation, and the answer is simple: they are not only seeking to accurately represent the Hebrew language, but they are also seeking to accurately convey it to native English speakers in the twenty-first century. Since the majority of people would have no idea what *cutting* a covenant" means, the translators wisely conveyed the broad idea with the phrase *"made* a covenant." This way, people are able to understand the Bible. But this also illustrates the value of Bible teachers and pastors learning Hebrew and Greek—the original languages in which the Bible was written. As they teach the word of God in their classrooms and churches, it is important that they be able to explain things like this.

So why does the Bible literally say that YHWH "cut a covenant" with Abram? Because in the ancient world, entering into a covenant involved the shedding of blood. Animals would be gathered and slaughtered and cut in half. It was a bloody affair! Each animal half would then be separated from its other half: half of a heifer on one side, and its other half on the other side. The same thing would happen to the goat and to the ram. This would create a bloody path between the animal halves. After this was set up, the covenant makers (or cutters) would swear a covenant oath, and they would each walk on the path between the animal halves. As they did so, they were saying with their actions, "If I do not hold up my side of this covenant, may it be done to me as has been done to these animals." To put it differently, they were absolutely committing to all the terms of the covenant and inviting a bloody death upon themselves if they did not comply.

A passage from the book of Jeremiah confirms this interpretation of the animal-halving symbolism:

The men who transgressed my covenant and did not keep the terms of the covenant that they made before me, I will make them like the calf that they cut in two and passed between its parts—the officials of Judah, the officials of Jerusalem, the eunuchs, the priests, and all the people of the land who passed between the parts of the calf. And I will give them into the hand of their enemies and into the hand of those who seek their lives. Their dead bodies shall be food for the birds of the air and the beasts of the earth. (Jer. 34:18–20)

Notice that the covenant breakers would be made like the animals they cut in two and that this would be accomplished by YHWH giving them into the hands of their enemies.[8] The curse of the covenant would come upon the covenant breakers.

As we return to Genesis 15, although both parties would usually walk between the cut-up animal pieces, in this covenant we read: "When the sun had gone down and it was dark, behold, a smoking fire pot and a flaming torch passed between these pieces" (v. 17). Although the imagery may escape us, the first readers of Genesis—the exodus generation, who were led by YHWH in a cloud by day and fire by night—would have immediately understood what was happening. The smoking fire pot (cf. "cloud") and the flaming torch (cf. "fire") represented YHWH himself walking between the animal halves. In this scene, YHWH was saying, "If this covenant is broken, may it be done to *me* as has been done to these bloody, slaughtered animals." Since Abram did not walk between the pieces, we can observe with Ray Vander Laan that YHWH was really saying, "If this covenant is broken, Abraham,

---

8 In fact, other cultures around Israel employed similar covenant-cutting ceremonies, with similar symbolic meaning. See Block, *Covenant*, 87–88.

for whatever reason—for My unfaithfulness or yours—I will pay the price. . . . If you or your descendants . . . fail to keep it, I will pay the price in blood."[9] Vander Laan then adds, "At that moment, Almighty God pronounced the death sentence on his Son Jesus."[10]

YHWH Establishes His Covenant with Abraham

As we move on to Genesis 17, we find more covenant language between YHWH and Abram. In this chapter, YHWH changed Abram's name to Abraham—Abram means "exalted father," and Abraham means "father of a multitude." In order to live up to his new name—in order for YHWH to be faithful to his promise— this ninety-nine-year-old man and his barren eighty-nine-year-old wife would need to have at least one son together. This helps to shed light on the sign of the covenant: circumcision. The sign was to be on the male organ of procreation in order to remind Abraham that there would be a son to come, and he would only come if God granted it.[11] And as the male descendants of Abraham—the Israelites—were circumcised, there would be a perpetual reminder of their dependence on God for the ultimate descendant of Abraham to come. Circumcision was a permanent marker, a private matter, that reminded God's Old Testament people that there was hope, and it was focused on a coming son from God.

---

9   Ray Vander Laan, *Echoes of His Presence: Stories of the Messiah from the People of His Day* (Colorado Springs, CO: Focus on the Family, 1996), 8–9, as cited in Gentry and Wellum, *Kingdom through Covenant*, 294.

10 Vander Laan, *Echoes of His Presence*, 8–9, as cited in Gentry and Wellum, *Kingdom through Covenant*, 294.

11 See Bruce K. Waltke and Cathi J. Fredricks, *Genesis: A Commentary* (Grand Rapids, MI: Zondervan, 2001), 264.

Although some Old Testament scholars believe this chapter tells the story of a *second* covenant between YHWH and Abraham,[12] Peter Gentry offers a different perspective based on the differences in wording between Genesis 15 and 17. We have seen that in Genesis 15, YHWH *cut* a covenant with Abram. Now in Genesis 17 we are told that YHWH *established* his covenant with Abraham. Gentry explains that the term "to cut a covenant" consistently refers to covenant initiation, and "to establish a covenant" means "'to affirm (verbally) the continued validity of a prior commitment'—that is, to affirm that one is still committed to the covenant relationship as established or initiated previously."[13] In line with this insight, we can observe that in Genesis 17, YHWH did not initiate a second covenant with Abraham. Instead, he affirmed his commitment to the covenant he had made previously in Genesis 15, even as he also added more details to it (e.g., circumcision as the sign of the covenant).

YHWH Swears an Oath to Abraham

Finally, in Genesis 22 YHWH asked Abraham to do the unthinkable: "Take your son, your only son Isaac, whom you love, and go to the land of Moriah, and offer him there as a burnt offering on one of the mountains of which I shall tell you" (v. 2). Although any parent would bristle at such a command, when we read it in the context of YHWH's covenant with Abraham, it actually gets worse: YHWH's promise to make Abraham a great nation was dependent on this one son who had finally been born to the elderly Abraham and Sarah. Therefore, YHWH was asking him

---

12 See, for example, T. Desmond Alexander, *From Paradise to the Promised Land: An Introduction to the Pentateuch*, 3rd ed. (Grand Rapids, MI: Baker Academic, 2012), 176–79.

13 Gentry and Wellum, *Kingdom through Covenant*, 187.

to sacrifice the very one through whom he would fulfill his covenant commitment.

The gripping scene unfolds with a trek up the mountain, the binding of Isaac, the raising of Abraham's hand to slaughter his son, and the glorious second command from YHWH: "Do not lay your hand on the boy or do anything to him, for now I know that you fear God, seeing you have not withheld your son, your only son, from me" (22:12). As the story continues, YHWH provided a ram for sacrifice in the place of Isaac, and then he swore an oath:

> By myself I have sworn, declares the LORD, because you have done this and have not withheld your son, your only son, I will surely bless you, and I will surely multiply your offspring as the stars of heaven and as the sand that is on the seashore. And your offspring shall possess the gate of his enemies, and in your offspring shall all the nations of the earth be blessed, because you have obeyed my voice. (22:16–18)

Notice that this solemn oath reiterated the covenant promises that YHWH had made previously to Abraham: in Genesis 12 YHWH called Abram; in Genesis 15 YHWH cut a covenant with Abram; in Genesis 17 YHWH established his covenant with Abraham; and in Genesis 22 YHWH reinforced his covenant with a solemn oath.

Zooming Out: YHWH's Covenants with His People

Now that we have zoomed in on one of the covenants between YHWH and his people, we can zoom out and look at the bigger picture. As we do so, we find six covenants. They can be summarized as follows:

Covenant Parties	Key Scriptures	Covenant Demands	Covenant Promises	Covenant Sign
YHWH and creation	Gen. 1:26–30; 2:15–25	Do not eat from the tree of the knowledge of good and evil	Life, abundance, presence of YHWH, harmony, no death	—
YHWH and Noah	Gen. 6:9–9:17	Build an ark and enter into it when YHWH tells you	YHWH will never again destroy all life by a flood	Rainbow
YHWH and Abraham	Gen. 12:1–9; 15:1–21; 17:1–27; 22:1–18	Go from your land and people to the place I will show you; be a blessing	A great people and an abundant land	Circumcision
YHWH and Moses/Israel	Ex. 19–24	Now that I have redeemed you, obey my instruction and live as my people	I will be your God and you will be my people	Sabbath
YHWH and David	2 Sam. 7	Do not abandon YHWH	A perpetual dynasty for David's son	—
A new covenant between YHWH and his people	Jer. 31:31–34; Ezek. 36:26–28	Obey YHWH from the heart	A new heart of flesh, on which the *torah* of YHWH will be written; indwelling by YHWH's Spirit; sins forgiven; all will know YHWH	—

Although each of these covenants does not necessarily include every aspect of YHWH's covenant with Abraham—calling, cutting, establishing, and oath—they all represent the same absolute guarantee of YHWH's faithfulness to his people.

YHWH's Covenants with Creation and with Noah

Since we have already zoomed in on the covenant with Abraham, and since we will spend an entire chapter on the covenant with Moses/Israel, in this place we will notice a few key elements of YHWH's covenants with creation and with Noah. Later, as we close this chapter by looking forward to Christ, we will consider the covenant with David, and the new covenant.

Although some scholars do not believe there was a covenant at creation, there is convincing evidence that suggests we should think of Genesis 1–2 in this way. To begin, we need to pay attention to the Bible's specific wording. The first time the word *covenant* occurs in the Bible is in Genesis 6:18—YHWH's covenant with Noah. However, a close look at the language reveals that YHWH did not *cut* a covenant in this verse; he *established* his covenant with Noah (see Gen. 6:18; 9:9, 11). By using this language, the Bible seems to suggest that YHWH was not *initiating* (or "cutting") a fresh covenant with Noah but upholding a previous covenant that had already been in place.

Next, we can notice the similarities between the covenant with Noah and the language used in the creation account. First, while the man and the woman were the crowning climax of creation, who were lavished with a new and fresh earth to inhabit, so Noah and his family were lavished with a re-created world to live in (Gen. 8:15–19). Then after Noah and his family exited the ark, they were given a blessing and a commission: "Be fruitful and multiply and fill the earth. The fear of you and the dread of you shall be upon every beast of the earth and upon every bird of the heavens, upon everything that creeps on the ground and all the fish of the sea. Into your hand they are delivered" (Gen. 9:1–2; cf. 9:7). This is essentially the same as the blessing and commission given to Adam: "Be fruitful and multiply and fill the earth and subdue it, and have dominion over the fish of the sea and over the birds of the heavens and over every living thing that moves on the earth" (Gen. 1:28). The giving of food was also similar, though at creation it was plants (Gen. 1:29), and Noah and his family were given meat as well (Gen. 9:3). Then comes the covenant:

> Then God said to Noah and to his sons with him, "Behold, I establish my covenant with you and your offspring after you, and with every living creature that is with you, the birds, the livestock, and every beast of the earth with you, as many as came out of the ark; it is for every beast of the earth. I establish my covenant with you, that never again shall all flesh be cut off by the waters of the flood, and never again shall there be a flood to destroy the earth." (Gen. 9:9–11)

The commitment was clear: God would never again destroy all flesh by a flood. But the parallels with creation, along with the fact that the covenant was "established" with Noah (and not "cut"), seem to point to the upholding of a previously initiated covenant at creation. Peter Gentry agrees, suggesting that although the word *covenant* is not used in Genesis 1:26–28; 2:4–3:24, the elements are present, because in these texts YHWH God initiated a relationship with his newly formed image bearers in connection to the newly formed creation.[14]

14 For a longer explanation of this, see Gentry and Wellum, *Kingdom through Covenant*, 211–58. I add that in light of this, it would be possible to group the covenants at creation and with

In this context, the next question is why the word *covenant* was not used at creation and why there was no animal cutting ceremony. The answer *could* be that there was not a covenant at creation after all, but an alternative answer is this: there was no need for a cutting ceremony before sin entered the world. Before sin, there was no disobedience, no death, no threats to covenant faithfulness. Therefore, the "cutting" of a covenant would have been *inappropriate* before the fall into sin. But the lavish blessings on the man and the woman, along with their restatement in the covenant with Noah, as well as the fact that the covenant was "established" with Noah, all seem to point to a covenant at creation. In fact, there are other places where the Bible describes a covenant without using the word. For example, in 2 Samuel 7 the word *covenant* is not used to describe YHWH's commitment to David, but as the later psalmists reflected on this event in Psalms 89 and 132, they used the word *covenant* to describe the scene.

This leads us to the big picture. Why did YHWH initiate a covenant at creation and then establish a covenant with Noah? The hint comes in Genesis 8:21–22. In the context of Noah's sacrifice to him, YHWH said, "I will never again curse the ground because of man, for the intention of man's heart is evil from his youth. Neither will I ever again strike down every living creature as I have done. While the earth remains, seedtime and harvest, cold and heat, summer and winter, day and night, shall not cease." In this promise, YHWH was saying that no matter what, no matter how

---

Noah together and so to identify five biblical covenants between YHWH and his people (instead of six): (1) creation/Noah; (2) Abraham; (3) Moses/Israel; (4) David; (5) new. This delineation is reflected in Jason S. DeRouchie, "Jesus' Bible: An Overview" in *What the Old Testament Authors Really Cared About: A Survey of Jesus' Bible*, ed. Jason S. DeRouchie (Grand Rapids, MI: Kregel Academic, 2013), 32.

faithful or unfaithful his people were, he would never again send a flood to destroy the earth (see also 9:11, 15).

We have already learned that creation is the theater of redemption. In this context, the flood tells the story of something horrifying: a de-creation. If the earth and its inhabitants were permanently destroyed, YHWH would have no theater (or people) with which (or whom) to accomplish his promise of Genesis 3:15. But YHWH faithfully *preserved* Noah and his family in the ark, and then he re-created the de-created world. Next, in his covenant with Noah YHWH effectively guaranteed that his re-creation, the new and fresh theater of redemption, would never again be destroyed.[15] This ensured that the coming Redeemer would have a world to enter, and a people to redeem.

Finally, the sign of the covenant with Noah is glorious. It may surprise some readers to discover that the Hebrew word usually translated "rainbow" simply means "bow," as in a weapon of war. In Genesis 9 YHWH literally said: "I have set my bow in the cloud, and it shall be a sign of the covenant between me and the earth. . . . When the bow is in the clouds, I will see it and remember the everlasting covenant between God and every living creature of all flesh that is on the earth" (vv. 13, 16). The imagery is glorious: in his covenant with Noah, YHWH was hanging up his weapon of war. No longer would he be at war with humanity, no longer would there be a threat of another flood to destroy the earth. Although it may or may not be pressing the image too far, some might even observe where the bow was pointed: into the heart of heaven. If this observation is valid, the imagery in YHWH's covenant with Noah would hint at the cost of YHWH's faithfulness to this covenant:

---

15 See Gentry and Wellum, *Kingdom through Covenant*, 208.

from a New Testament perspective, we can say that it was aimed at the heart of his beloved Son.

Looking Forward to Christ:
The New Covenant in Jesus's Blood

After the covenants at creation and with Noah and Abraham, the next were with Moses/Israel (Ex. 19–24), and then with David (2 Sam. 7).[16] In the covenant with David, YHWH promised that David's son would reign on his throne forever (2 Sam. 7:16). This promise hearkens back to the blessing of Judah, that his descendant would carry a ruler's staff/scepter (Gen. 49:10). In time, though, a crisis occurred: Solomon's temple was destroyed, no king sat on David's throne, and God's people were taken out of their land into Babylonian exile. Although there was a later return from exile and a rebuilding of a second temple under the leadership of Ezra, there was still no king on David's throne, and God's people were still ultimately ruled by foreign superpowers. It was in this context, when Israel had no king, that Jesus was born as King of the Jews (Matt. 2:2) and would later be mocked as King of the Jews (27:29) before he died as King of the Jews (27:37).

Before the arrest, trial, humiliation, and death of Jesus, we find another important covenant scene. On the night that Jesus was betrayed, he ate a Passover meal with his disciples. In that scene, Jesus took bread, gave thanks, broke it, and said, "This is my body, which is for you. Do this in remembrance of me" (1 Cor. 11:24). After supper he took the cup and added: "This cup is the new covenant in my blood. Do this, as often as you drink it, in remembrance of me" (11:25). In light of our study of covenants, this passage is

---

16 Since we will spend an entire chapter on YHWH's covenant with Moses/Israel, we will not discuss it further in this place.

telling. Jesus was saying that he, in that moment, was initiating the new covenant that had been promised in the Old Testament (see Jer. 31; Ezek. 36). In line with covenants in the Old Testament, this one would also be initiated by blood, only the new covenant would witness the pouring out of *Jesus's* blood. In the act of dying on the cross for our sins, Jesus was the covenant sacrifice. Sandra L. Richter has put it beautifully once again:

> Do you hear the echo of Exodus 24? Moses said, "this is the blood of the covenant"; Jesus said, "this is My blood of the covenant." This echo is not coincidental, nor was it missed by its first-century audience. Rather, on that Passover night Jesus announced to his disciples that something greater than the exodus was about to transpire. By means of oath and sacrifice, another rabble of slaves was about to be transformed into God's covenant-people (cf. 1 Pet 2:10). As Moses sprinkled the blood of bulls upon the people of Israel in order to ratify the Sinai covenant, so Jesus distributed his own blood that night to ratify a new covenant. And this time the oaths were not sealed by "the blood of bulls and goats and the ashes of a heifer," but by the blood of God the Son (cf. Heb 9:13–15). Moreover, the slaves who were freed from their bondage by this new covenant were not delivered merely from Egypt, but from death itself. Thus we see that the safe and structured communion meal that you and I participate in according to our liturgies and traditions is actually a most abbreviated representation of the ratification of the new covenant. And in this new covenant the Lord of the cosmos has served as both suzerain and sacrifice.[17]

---

17 Richter, *The Epic of Eden*, 89. As noted in this chapter's note 3, the term *suzerain* will be further explained on pp. 135–36, 190–91.

What a gospel! No wonder the apostle Paul added that every time we participate in the Lord's Supper at church, we "proclaim the Lord's death until he comes" (1 Cor. 11:26). In other words, as we participate in the Lord's Supper, our actions preach the gospel.

Discussion Questions

1. What are some Old Testament examples of a covenant between human parties?

2. How would you define the word *covenant*?

3. In the Old Testament, what is the difference between cutting a covenant and establishing a covenant?

4. Explain the significance of cutting animals in half when a covenant was initiated.

5. Explain the significance of the smoking fire pot and flaming torch passing between the animal halves in Genesis 15.

6. What are the key promises of YHWH's covenant with Abram?

7. Was a covenant given at creation? Give reasons to support your answer.

8. How does YHWH's covenant with Noah relate to his big-picture plan of the redemption of a people for himself?

5

Exodus

Redemption Accomplished
(and Foreshadowed)

IT WOULD BE UNBELIEVABLE if it had not been a direct intervention from God: an entire nation of slaves who had lived and
multiplied and served in Egypt for four hundred years was freed.
Centuries of chains were broken. Forced labor ceased. And as this
nation exited out of Egypt with their former captors in hot pursuit,
the waters of the Red Sea were parted in two so they could pass
through on dry land. After their safe arrival on the other side, those
same waters engulfed Pharaoh and his army.

When YHWH ushered Israel out of Egypt—an event referred
to as "the exodus" throughout the Bible—he accomplished the
greatest act of redemption in the entire Old Testament. It makes
sense, then, that centuries later, when God's people were in
desperate circumstances once again, the prophets envisioned
their coming deliverance as a *second exodus*. Later still, the New

Testament authors and Jesus himself cast his work of redemption as the ultimate fulfillment of the second exodus the prophets had promised. Kenneth J. Turner put it this way: "The exodus is to the Old Testament what the cross-resurrection event is to the New Testament. In each case, the great redemptive act (exodus/cross) produces the covenant community of God's people (Israel/church) who are called to serve God and his universal mission."[1] In light of these things, we can conclude that *in order to understand the message of the Bible, we need to understand Israel's exodus from Egyptian slavery.*

In this chapter we will focus on the most important features of the exodus from Egypt as they are recorded in the first eighteen chapters of the book of Exodus. Since we have already painted something of a picture of this deliverance in this book's introduction, we are able to focus on key passages. We'll begin by considering the promised, distant exodus. Then we'll overview the coming, imminent exodus. Finally, we'll see the exodus as redemption accomplished before we close by considering the exodus of Jesus.

The Promised, Distant Exodus

We have seen that the Bible's story is an epic of redemption, an account of YHWH delivering a people from sin and to himself. We have also said that the greatest act of redemption in the Old Testament was the exodus from Egypt, and that this theme of salvation-as-exodus reverberates through the rest of the Bible. It makes sense, then, that the first promise of the exodus took place long before the book of Exodus began. In fact, it occurred roughly four hundred years prior to the exodus from Egypt.

---

1   Kenneth J. Turner, "Exodus," in *What the Old Testament Authors Really Cared About: A Survey of Jesus' Bible*, ed. Jason S. DeRouchie (Grand Rapids, MI: Kregel Academic, 2013), 89.

In the context of YHWH cutting his covenant with Abram in Genesis 15, a clear promise was made about the future of the patriarch's family lineage:

> As the sun was going down, a deep sleep fell on Abram. And behold, dreadful and great darkness fell upon him. Then the LORD said to Abram, "Know for certain that your offspring will be sojourners in a land that is not theirs and will be servants there, and they will be afflicted for four hundred years. But I will bring judgment on the nation that they serve, and afterward they shall come out with great possessions. As for you, you shall go to your fathers in peace; you shall be buried in a good old age. And they shall come back here in the fourth generation, for the iniquity of the Amorites is not yet complete." (Gen. 15:12–16)

This is a very clear promise of a coming exodus for the descendants of Abram, before they were even born, much less enslaved. But why did it come in the context of YHWH's covenant with the patriarch? Because in this covenant YHWH promised, "To your offspring I give this land, from the river of Egypt to the great river, the river Euphrates, the land of the Kenites, the Kenizzites, the Kadmonites, the Hittites, the Perizzites, the Rephaim, the Amorites, the Canaanites, the Girgashites and the Jebusites" (15:18–21).

In short, Abram would become a great nation, and that nation would possess the land of his sojournings. We can imagine that without the promise of a coming deliverance from slavery, God's people would *feel* abandoned by him. But in the covenant with Abram, he predicted that deliverance would come. In fact, he also explained why deliverance would be delayed by four hundred years: the iniquity of the nations who inhabited Canaan was not yet complete. We can picture a glass slowly filling up with drops of water. It may take a long time, but eventually the cup will fill to overflowing. In a similar way, the cup of YHWH's wrath would be poured out only when it was filled to overflowing, when a watching cosmos would see his judgment on these nations as an awesome act of justice. Deliverance would come for his people, but it would be reserved for a future date.

The Coming, Imminent Exodus

A Bleak but Hopeful Situation

Over the next few decades, Abraham's descendants were traced to the fourth generation, through Isaac, Jacob, and then Jacob's twelve sons. By the end of Genesis, the twelve brothers were rescued from famine through respite in Egypt. Although they were safe, Egypt was never a good destination in Genesis—it had been where God's people went when their faith was waning (e.g., Gen. 12:10–20). Could it be that Egypt would also be the location of their coming slavery (Gen. 15:13)?

The book of Exodus begins with a list of seventy descendants of Abraham who had joined Joseph in Egypt. On the one hand, the promise to Abraham was clearly reaching fruition: "But the people of Israel were fruitful and increased greatly; they multiplied and grew exceedingly strong, so that the land was filled with them" (Ex. 1:7). God was definitely working to accomplish his promises. On the other hand, in order to get to the redemption of these people, careful Bible readers know that the situation for Abraham's descendants would get much worse before it got gloriously better. Therefore, it shouldn't surprise us to find that "a new king" came on the throne "over Egypt, who did not know Joseph" (1:8).

The situation very quickly became horrible, as God's people were abused as slaves. However, "the more they were oppressed, the more they multiplied and the more they spread abroad" (1:12). As careful readers, we can clearly see evidence that God's covenant faithfulness to Abraham was on full display; oppressors could make their lives miserable, but their God was unstoppable—despite their oppressed state, he was making his people as numerous as the stars (cf., e.g., Gen. 15:5).

The Egyptians intuitively felt threatened by this multiplication of the Israelites, so they made the lives of their slaves more miserable with ruthless forced labor. In fact, the king of Egypt decreed infanticide, ordering the Egyptian midwives, "When you serve as midwife to the Hebrew women and see them on the birthstool, if it is a son, you shall kill him, but if it is a daughter, she shall live" (Ex. 1:16). But these midwives feared God and disobeyed orders, even lying to Pharaoh in order to preserve these young lives. In response, Pharaoh issued a new order: "Every son that is born to the Hebrews you shall *cast into the Nile*, but you shall let every daughter live" (1:22). Although this type of oppression of a people group is always horrendously wrong, Ross Blackburn reminds us to step back and remember the big-picture story of the Pentateuch. As we do so, we recall that the descendants of Abraham were ultimately going to be a means of making YHWH known globally (Gen. 12:1–3). Therefore, "Pharaoh's opposition threatens God's purposes to be known throughout the world."[2] In other words, Pharaoh was challenging YHWH's promised global redemption.

---

2   W. Ross Blackburn, *The God Who Makes Himself Known: The Missionary Heart of the Book of Exodus*, New Studies in Biblical Theology 28, ed. D. A. Carson (Downers Grove, IL: InterVarsity, 2012), 30.

The Birth and Preparation of a Redeemer

In this difficult but hopeful context, we learn about the birth of a baby in the lineage of Levi (Ex. 2:1). His mother was able to hide him from Pharaoh's murderous orders for three months, but when it became impossible to continue concealing him, she made a little "ark"—some readers may want to turn back to this book's introduction to reread the explanation of this word choice—and set him adrift on the mighty Nile. Not only did the child survive, but he was found by Pharaoh's daughter, who *paid* the baby's mother to nurse him (2:9). After the time of nursing was complete, his mom brought him back to Pharaoh's daughter, and he became her son. Pharaoh's daughter named him Moses because she drew him out of the water—the name Moses is a wordplay on a Hebrew verb that means "to draw out." From the perspective of Pharaoh's daughter, Moses was named because she "drew him out" of the mighty Nile River, but from the perspective of the reader of the book of Exodus, we know that this baby would later "draw Israel out" of Egypt through the water.[3]

So the first forty years of Moses's life were spent in Egypt. Although the Bible does not share details about the bulk of his upbringing, it certainly implies that he would have had privileged access to the best of everything, including education.[4] Egypt was the world superpower, and Moses was raised in the house of its Pharaoh. However, when he was forty Moses witnessed an Egyptian beating a Hebrew man. Moses quickly killed the Egyptian and hid his body in the sand—although he would one day be a deliverer of God's

---

3   See W. Hall Harris, ed., *NET Bible Notes*, 2nd ed., Accordance electronic ed. (Garland, TX: Biblical Studies Press, 2019), Ex. 2:10, n. 36.

4   As Stephen later put it, "Moses was instructed in all the wisdom of the Egyptians, and he was mighty in his words and deeds" (Acts 7:22).

people, in this instance he was attempting deliverance in his own way and in his own timing. When word got out, Moses fled from Egypt, met a priest's daughter, and *saved* her flock from shepherds who had driven them away, thus *delivering* the shepherdess from her distress. Moses then married that woman, and together they started a family. Although especially the first scene shows a humanly devised way of delivering, in both of these scenes—seeking to rescue a Hebrew man in his distress, and saving a flock and delivering a shepherdess from her distress—Exodus 2 hints toward the future redemption YHWH would accomplish by means of Moses.

As Exodus 2 draws to a close, the desperation of God's people continued: "During those many days the king of Egypt died, and the people of Israel groaned because of their slavery and cried out for help" (v. 23). Although the first two chapters of Exodus can be read in a few minutes, forty years passed in chapter 2 alone. The intensity of the suffering had been constant, and the need for redemption was acute. This makes the closing words of the chapter even more glorious. In Exodus 2:23–25 we learn first that their cry for rescue *came up* to God, and God *heard* their groaning. In other words, the God to whom they cried was not a distant deity who failed to hear. They had been crying out for decades, centuries even, but their God *did* hear them.

Next, God *remembered* his covenant with Abraham, Isaac, and Jacob. In the Bible, when God remembers, he is not calling to mind something he had forgotten. Instead, the God who never forgets is acting on something. And as readers of the Pentateuch, we understand that the word *covenant* was God's guarantee of redemption, and that his covenant with Abraham—extended through his sons, Isaac and Jacob—involved the guarantee of an enormous nation who would settle in the land of Canaan. In Exodus 1 we witnessed the growth of this nation in the face of relentless Egyptian mistreatment. Now at the close of Exodus 2, we are being pointed to a resolution for their need of a land of their own.

Finally, the chapter concludes by summarizing that "God *saw* the people of Israel—and God knew" (2:25). Not only did Israel's God witness the events of their mistreatment, but he also *knew*—a Hebrew verb that speaks of his intimate acquaintance with their suffering. In summary, God was attentive, his covenant with Abraham was at the forefront of his mind, and he was intimately acquainted with his people's need. Something big was about to happen.

The Call of a Redeemer and the Name of YHWH

Although Exodus 3 continues the fast-paced story leading up to the exodus from Egypt, from the perspective of the characters in the drama, time was moving slowly. While Exodus 2 began with the birth of Moses, by the end of the chapter he was a forty-year-old husband and father. And while Exodus 3 continues the story, forty more years passed and the eighty-year-old Moses had been serving as his father-in-law's shepherd for four whole decades. This was quite a demotion—one who had been raised in luxury and power for his first forty years then lived in obscurity and humble circumstances for another forty years.

It was in this wilderness that YHWH appeared to Moses in a burning bush. And then he spoke: "Do not come near; take your sandals off your feet, for the place on which you are standing is holy ground. . . . I am the God of your father, the God of Abraham, the God of Isaac, and the God of Jacob" (3:5–6). In response, "Moses hid his face, for he was afraid to look at God." What followed was the promise of redemption: YHWH was going to act to deliver his people now; he would bring them to the land previously promised to Abraham, and he would do it through Moses (3:7–10).

After a bit more conversation, Moses asked God his name; he wanted to know what to say if Israel asked. But Bruce Waltke points out that a close look at the Hebrew wording reveals that Moses was asking for more than God's name as a label—he was asking for the meaning of his name.[5] In response, we read these great words:

> God said to Moses, "I AM WHO I AM." And he said, "Say this to the people of Israel: 'I AM has sent me to you.'" God also said to Moses, "Say this to the people of Israel: 'The LORD, the God of your fathers, the God of Abraham, the God of Isaac, and the God of Jacob, has sent me to you.' This is my name forever, and thus I am to be remembered throughout all generations. (3:14–15)

How are we to understand this passage? First, the Hebrew verb translated "I AM" literally means "I will be," and the name YHWH literally means "he will be." While YHWH referred to himself as "I will be," others would refer to him as "he will be"—YHWH (translated as "the LORD" in most English Bibles). The name carried connotations of the never-changing, always-faithful nature of God; he would be tomorrow what he was today, and his people could therefore count on him.

Next, in a later scene YHWH spoke about his name again: "God spoke to Moses and said to him, 'I am the LORD. I appeared to Abraham, to Isaac, and to Jacob, as God Almighty, but by my name the LORD I did not make myself known to them'" (6:2–3). Although this may sound at first like the name YHWH had not been revealed until

5   See Bruce K. Waltke and Charles Yu, *An Old Testament Theology: An Exegetical, Canonical, and Thematic Approach* (Grand Rapids, MI: Zondervan, 2007), 365.

this point in history, it actually appears 165 times in the book of Genesis. In that book people called on his name (e.g., Gen. 4:26), and YHWH identified himself by this name (e.g., Gen. 15:7). Just as insights from the Hebrew language revealed that Moses had been asking for the *meaning* of YHWH's name in Exodus 3:13, more insights reveal that in Exodus 6:2–3, the *significance* of his name, YHWH, had never been fully understood until what was about to transpire.[6] Therefore, since this name was revealed in the context of the greatest act of redemption in the entire Old Testament, it was associated with his covenant faithfulness.

J. A. Motyer's translation of this verse is helpful: "God spoke to Moses, and said to him: I am Yahweh. And I showed myself to Abraham, to Isaac, and to Jacob in the character of *El Shaddai*, but in the character expressed by my name Yahweh I did not make myself known to them."[7] The people of the Genesis drama did not have a chance to grasp this name in its fullness, because they had not yet experienced *redemption*. Although they knew and used this name, they didn't really understand its full import, so they knew him primarily as *El Shaddai* (God Almighty). But beginning with Moses and the people of Israel who would experience the exodus from Egypt, the meaning and significance of the name YHWH was understood and *experienced*. His personal, covenant name would become the primary way his people would refer to him.

Now that the human redeemer had been identified and called, and now that the meaning and significance of YHWH's name had been revealed, it was time for action. And that is exactly what happens next in the drama.

---

6 See Waltke and Yu, *Old Testament Theology*, 365.
7 J. A. Motyer, *The Revelation of the Divine Name* (London: Tyndale, 1959), 12. As cited in Blackburn, *The God Who Makes Himself Known*, 27.

The Exodus: Redemption Accomplished

The Plagues

As Exodus 3 closes, Moses was told by YHWH to go back to Egypt and gather the elders of Israel to announce: (1) the appearance of YHWH; (2) their coming deliverance from Egypt; and (3) their coming deliverance to the promised land. The repetition of "the LORD, the God of your fathers, the God of Abraham, of Isaac, and of Jacob" (e.g., Ex. 3:16) not only emphasized continuity between the God of the exodus with the God of the forefathers of Israel; it also called to mind the covenant promises of YHWH—especially of Israel as a great nation who would possess the land of Abraham's sojournings.

YHWH continued by telling Moses that Moses would gain a hearing with the king of Egypt, to whom he would appeal to let YHWH's people go a three days' journey into the wilderness to sacrifice to him (3:18). But YHWH also revealed to Moses that the king of Egypt would not let Israel go unless compelled by the mighty hand of YHWH, so that is exactly what would happen—YHWH would strike Egypt with wonders, and the king of Egypt would let YHWH's people go (Ex. 3:19–20). In fact, on their way out YHWH would give Israel favor in the sight of the Egyptians—they would be given silver, gold, and clothing as they left (3:21–22). And so the stage was set for the exodus from Egypt.

With Aaron as his spokesman, Moses returned to Egypt, gathered the elders of Israel, and reported the words of YHWH to them. Moses also did miraculous signs in the sight of the people to prove he was the legitimate deliverer from YHWH (Ex. 4). The people believed, so they bowed their heads and worshiped (4:31). Next, Moses and Aaron gained an audience with Pharaoh and appealed, "Thus says the LORD, the God of Israel, 'Let my people go, that they may hold a feast to me in the wilderness'" (Ex. 5:1). What followed was an exchange that would be repeated over numerous chapters: Pharaoh refused, YHWH sent plagues on Egypt, Pharaoh was humbled and asked Moses to pray to YHWH to relent, the plague was lifted, and Pharaoh hardened his heart and refused to let God's people go. And the cycle was repeated ten times.

In the first chapter of this book, we noticed that the plagues on Egypt represented a temporary, localized, and partial return to precreation chaos. John Currid's chart adds depth to our link between the various plagues on Egypt and the creation narrative:[8]

Creation Day	Description	Plague on Egypt	Description
Day 1: Gen. 1:3–5	Light created out of darkness	Plague 9: Ex. 10:21–29	Darkness prevailing over the light
Day 2: Gen. 1:6–8	Waters ordered and separated	Plague 1: Ex. 7:15–25	Chaos by changing water to blood
Day 3: Gen. 1:9–13	Dry land and vegetation appear	Plagues 7–8: Ex. 9:13–10:20	Destruction of vegetation
Day 4: Gen. 1:14–19	Creation of the luminaries	Plague 9: Ex. 10:21–29	Darkening of the luminaries
Day 5: Gen. 1:20–23	Creation of birds, fish, and sea life	Plagues 1–2: Ex. 7:15–8:15	Death of fish and frogs
Day 6: Gen. 1:24–31	Creation of animals and humans	Plagues 3–6: Ex. 8:16–9:12 Plague 10: Ex. 11:1–12:51	Plague of insects, anthrax, boils on beasts and humans; killing of firstborn

8   Excerpted from John D. Currid, "Exodus," in *A Biblical-Theological Introduction to the Old Testament: The Gospel Promised*, ed. Miles Van Pelt (Wheaton, IL: Crossway, 2016), 79. This figure first appeared in John D. Currid, *Ancient Egypt and the Old Testament* (Grand Rapids, MI: Baker Academic, 1997), 115, fig. 3. Used by permission.

The connection is certainly clear! In the plagues, YHWH was flexing his muscles—or to use the biblical language, his hand was outstretched—and showing the Egyptians (and a watching people of Israel) that the God of the Hebrews was also the God of creation. Since YHWH held the power over all the wealth and abundance and power of Egypt, if Egypt would continue to suppress and oppress his people, he would gain victory over them.

In the first chapter of this book, we also saw that the ten plagues were a full frontal attack on the so-called gods of Egypt. By way of reminder, Egypt worshiped the sun god, Re. But YHWH not only created the sun (Gen. 1); he could also cause darkness to prevail in the land (Ex. 10:21). Likewise, if Pharaoh was worshiped as a god, and his firstborn son would soon ascend to the same heights, YHWH would put that same firstborn son to death (11:5). YHWH would have no rivals! This negative "against the gods of Egypt" purpose of the plagues was also related to the positive "YHWH deserves all worship" purpose that is summarized through the plagues story in words such as these: ". . . that you may know that I am the LORD" (e.g., 10:2).[9]

As the story of the plagues on Egypt progresses, careful readers will notice a subtle shift. While Pharaoh hardened his own heart during the early plagues (e.g., 8:32), later on YHWH hardened Pharaoh's heart (e.g., 9:12). Although at first glance this may seem unfair to twenty-first-century readers, Bruce Waltke makes a helpful point: "Through hardening Pharaoh's heart, the Moral Governor of the universe shows that he rules creation and history and deals with the creation according to his moral pleasure,

9   For a more in-depth discussion on the plagues as directly confronting the gods of Egypt, see especially L. Michael Morales, *Exodus Old and New*, Essential Studies in Biblical Theology 2, ed. Benjamin L. Gladd (Downers Grove, IL: IVP Academic, 2020), 45.

determining how long he will extend his grace and varying the degrees and kinds of judgments he inflicts."[10] By the end of the plagues story, Pharaoh was humbled and devastated, and Israel was free to leave. But before we move on, the final plague deserves a bit more attention.

The Tenth Plague: The Death of the Firstborn and the Passover

After nine cycles of plague and hardening, the tenth was the most severe and sobering: every firstborn son in Egypt would die on a single night. Although this horrible plague resulted from Pharaoh's repeated refusals—nine times!—to let Israel go, it was also in view from the beginning. At the time of Moses's call and commissioning, before he even entered Egypt, we read:

> And the LORD said to Moses, "When you go back to Egypt, see that you do before Pharaoh all the miracles that I have put in your power. But I will harden his heart, so that he will not let the people go. Then you shall say to Pharaoh, 'Thus says the LORD, Israel is my firstborn son, and I say to you, "Let my son go that he may serve me." If you refuse to let him go, behold, I will kill your firstborn son.'" (4:21–23)

Since Israel as a people group was the firstborn of YHWH, failure to let them go would result in death for the firstborn sons of Egypt. In fact, the devastation would reach from the highest to the lowest people, and even to the livestock of Egypt: "Every firstborn in the land of Egypt shall die, from the firstborn of Pharaoh who sits on his throne, even to the firstborn of the slave girl who is behind

10   Waltke and Yu, *Old Testament Theology*, 380.

the handmill, and all the firstborn of the cattle" (11:5). However, things would be markedly different for Israel: "But not a dog shall growl against any of the people of Israel, either man or beast, that you may know that the LORD makes a distinction between Egypt and Israel" (11:7). The firstborn of YHWH, with whom he was in covenant, would not experience death on this terrible night.

Exodus 12 tells the story of the Passover feast, which would become an annual event in the Jewish calendar. That night, the head of each Israelite household slaughtered a lamb without blemish and painted its blood on the doorpost of their house. The lamb was then prepared for a family meal, along with unleavened bread that did not have time to rise before baking. And it was cooked with bitter herbs to remind them of the bitterness of their life in Egypt. Also, the family was fully clothed and ready to leave Egypt quickly as they ate—because they might have been called upon to leave at any moment. Everything about this meal was one of haste. But the blood of the lamb was also a reminder that the very picture of purity and innocence had to die in order for the people to escape from the horrors of death on this night. Israel was spared death, not because of her righteousness, but because she was covered by the blood of something innocent. The ensuing scene was sobering:

> At midnight the LORD struck down all the firstborn in the land of Egypt, from the firstborn of Pharaoh who sat on his throne to the firstborn of the captive who was in the dungeon, and all the firstborn of the livestock. And Pharaoh rose up in the night, he and all his servants and all the Egyptians. And there was a great cry in Egypt, for there was not a house where someone was not dead. (12:29–30)

In the face of this, YHWH called Israel to leave: they were now free; the descendants of Abraham were a mighty nation, and they would soon enter the land YHWH had promised.

The Exit and the Red Sea

In a surprising turn of events, YHWH led Israel out of Egypt and into what looked like a trap as Pharaoh and his army pressed Israel against a body of water. But the trap would not be for them; it would be for the Egyptians:

> "For Pharaoh will say of the people of Israel, 'They are wandering in the land; the wilderness has shut them in.' And I will harden Pharaoh's heart, and he will pursue them, and I will get glory over Pharaoh and all his host, and the Egyptians shall know that I am the LORD." And they did so. (14:3–4)

Many of us are familiar with the story: YHWH caused the water of the Red Sea to part, Israel passed through on dry ground, and when Pharaoh and his army followed, YHWH caused the water to engulf and drown them. In response, "Israel saw the great power that the LORD used against the Egyptians, so the people feared the LORD, and they believed in the LORD and in his servant Moses" (14:31).

Provision in the Desert

Before we close, we need to notice that YHWH did not cause Israel to escape aimlessly—he pointed them to Sinai. The story of this journey is told in Exodus 15:22–18:27, and in it they were completely dependent on YHWH as they traveled through a barren desert. Along the way he provided food (e.g., Ex. 16) and water (e.g., 15:22–27). And in each time of desperation, we witness the theme of a grumbling people and the abundant provision of their God.

The story of food is most encouraging, as YHWH rained down bread from heaven for the people each day (16:4). Other than the day before the Sabbath, they were not allowed to gather more than was needed for a single day so that they would be consciously dependent on YHWH every day. On the first morning of this "harvest," the people asked each other, "What is it?" (or in Hebrew, *man hu*) and the name stuck: the people would harvest "what is it" ("manna") six mornings per week for forty years. YHWH provides! Then at the beginning of Exodus 19, Israel arrived at the wilderness of Sinai. YHWH's people were now free to worship him. Just as YHWH called Abram in Genesis 12, long before he cut a covenant with him in Genesis 15, so YHWH delivered Israel, setting the stage for a formal covenant. That will be the topic of our next chapter.

Looking Forward to Christ: The Exodus of Jesus

At the beginning of this chapter, we noticed that the theme of exodus reverberates through the rest of the Bible. Hundreds of years later, when Israel had a land, a temple, and a king, they were divided in two and then defeated by the opposing Assyrian and Babylonian armies. Their land was taken, their goods plundered, and the people were exiled to a foreign land. In the face of this, the prophets promised restoration for repentance under the terms of the covenant, and the coming restoration for Israel was cast as a second exodus (e.g., Isa. 11:11–16). Although Israel would eventually be given their land back, and although they did rebuild the temple, they never experienced the fullness promised in the prophets—the full second exodus had not yet been accomplished.

In light of this, it makes sense that the New Testament authors cast the work of Jesus as a second exodus. Although hints of restoration were initiated in the Old Testament and the time between the testaments, it was not until the cross and resurrection that the true second exodus—the bigger and better and ultimate deliverance from sin and all of its effects—was accomplished. This is seen in the Last Supper, the meal Jesus ate with his disciples on the night he was betrayed. As we saw in the previous chapter, Jesus declared the cup to be the new covenant in his blood. While the disciples ate this Passover meal with Jesus, they were learning that the ultimate sacrifice for the ultimate Passover was sitting with them. In fact, they were about to learn what it meant to have their sins covered by the blood of the ultimate sinless one!

Another significant second-exodus passage is found in the Gospel of Luke. Many of us will recall the story of the transfiguration of Jesus—when his glory was revealed on the mountain, his face was altered, and his clothes became dazzling white (Luke 9:29). After this, Moses and Elijah appeared and spoke with Jesus of his departure, which he was about to accomplish at Jerusalem (Luke 9:30). While it may seem strange for the coming death and resurrection of Jesus to be described as his "departure," the word in the original Greek adds insight: literally, Jesus and Moses and Elijah were talking about Jesus's coming *exodus*. According to the Gospel of Luke, in the death and resurrection of Jesus, the ultimate exodus was about to take place; the first exodus therefore foreshadowed this more ultimate act of redemption. Sin would be paid for, Satan would be conquered, and death would be swallowed up in victory. The exodus of Jesus was the true exodus in which the hope promised in the Old Testament was finally fulfilled, and all who are "in Christ"—who trust him as Savior and follow him as Lord—receive something better than the first exodus would ever accomplish: citizenship as God's people in a new heavens and new earth *forever*. What a glorious gospel!

Discussion Questions

1. The author suggested that in order to understand the message of the Bible, we need to understand Israel's exodus out of Egypt. What reasons did he give for this claim?

2. What are some ways Exodus 1–2 reveals that in the midst of his people's suffering, YHWH was faithfully fulfilling the promises he made in his covenant with Abraham?

3. When the Bible tells us that YHWH "remembered" something, what does it mean? Did he forget and recall that thing, or is there a better explanation?

4. According to Exodus 3 and 6, what is the meaning and significance of YHWH's name?

5. The author shared a few New Testament passages about the exodus of Jesus. Can you think of any others that hint that Jesus's work on the cross accomplished a second exodus for God's people?

6

Torah

Living as the Redeemed

WHY DO WE NEED TO SPEND a chapter focusing on a bunch of ancient laws, when the New Testament so clearly teaches that Christians are saved by grace alone through faith alone? When Christians think about the Ten Commandments, for example, what often comes to mind is a legalistic Old Testament code that stands in contrast to the grace offered to new-covenant believers in Jesus. However, as we look at these commandments in context, we begin to see that this is not the case. For those who lived in Old Testament times, the demands of the law arrived in a context of grace. Not only this, but when we look forward from these grace-surrounded demands of the law to Christ, we are led to experience some glorious aspects of the gospel in a much deeper way. All of a sudden, studying a bunch of ancient laws has become very practical. In this chapter we will focus on YHWH's covenant with Moses/Israel (Ex. 19–24) as well as the account of the golden calf and the revelation of YHWH's compassionate character (Ex. 32–34). But before we do this, let's get oriented by looking at some big-picture details.

Approaching Sinai

Although several of the Old Testament place names will be unfamiliar to modern readers, the name "Sinai" may sound vaguely recognizable. This is because Mount Sinai was the location where Moses received the Ten Commandments. When we notice the details of the story of the Pentateuch, however, we see that Sinai—the mountain and its surrounding region—was of central importance. In Exodus 19:1 we are told that Israel came *to* the wilderness of Sinai a few months after the exodus from Egypt. Then in Numbers 10:12 we read that "the people of Israel set out by stages *from* the wilderness of Sinai." This means that the central portion of the Pentateuch took place at Sinai.

In fact, sixty-eight chapters occur before the arrival of Israel at the wilderness of Sinai, and sixty chapters follow the departure of Israel from the wilderness of Sinai. In the middle, the fifty-nine chapters from Exodus 19 to Numbers 10 take place at Sinai. Alternatively, we can think of the centrality of Sinai in terms of the journey out of Egypt: Israel stayed in six locations before arriving at Sinai, and another six afterward.[1]

In this book's introduction we noticed that although Christians most often refer to the first five books of the Old Testament as "the Pentateuch," the Bible itself refers to this section as "the book of Moses." This reminds us that these five books tell a single story. Therefore, it is legitimate to break the material up into three chunks,

---

1   See L. Michael Morales, *Who Shall Ascend the Mountain of the Lord? A Biblical Theology of the Book of Leviticus*, New Studies in Biblical Theology 37, ed. D. A. Carson (Downers Grove, IL: InterVarsity Press, 2015), 86.

even though it is also separated into five books. And once again, the important message from this three-chunk breakup is this: in the story of the Pentateuch, Sinai is central.[2]

At the beginning of the Sinai portion of the Pentateuch, Exodus 19–24 tells the story of YHWH's covenant with Moses/Israel. A name is even given to these six chapters: in Exodus 24:7 they are called "the Book of the Covenant." This cluster of chapters begins with Israel's arrival at the wilderness of Sinai in Exodus 19:1 and leads to the summit of Mount Sinai and back again. As we notice the details of these chapters, we will see that they begin with grace, continue with grace, and conclude with grace.

Since Exodus 19–24 is called "the Book of the Covenant," and these chapters are also the account of YHWH's covenant with Moses/Israel, we will notice that they do not tell the story of how to *become* God's people. After all, they occur after the greatest act of redemption in the entire Old Testament—the exodus from Egypt. In fact, the tone of these chapters is something like this: now that you are YHWH's redeemed people, his treasured possession, this is how you are to live and behave and order your community life.

There is one more important feature of these chapters to consider before we dive in. One reason Christians often have a negative view of the Old Testament laws is just that: the English word *law* most often calls to mind legalistic rules that need to be obeyed. In the English Old Testament, *law* is the most common translation for the Hebrew word *torah*. However, *torah* is a word that does not have an exact English counterpart—anyone who has learned to speak a second language understands that the fullness of a word's

---

2   I first learned this insight from Stephen G. Dempster, *Dominion and Dynasty: A Theology of the Hebrew Bible*, New Studies in Biblical Theology 15, ed. D. A. Carson (Downers Grove, IL: InterVarsity Press, 2003), 100.

meaning can sometimes get lost in translation. In this case, the Hebrew word *torah* carries a positive tone. For this reason, if I am reading an English translation of the Bible and I encounter the word *law*, I find it helpful to read it as *instruction*, or even just *torah*, to remind myself of the positive tone of the Hebrew word. With this in mind, we are ready to notice some of the key features of Exodus 19–24.

Grace and Instruction at the Summit of Mount Sinai

Grace and Instruction in YHWH's First Words to Israel

As the scene at Sinai begins, we read that "Israel encamped *before* the mountain, while Moses *went up* to God" (Ex. 19:2–3). This means that Israel came to the foot of the mountain. However, did you notice that the text does not say that Moses went up the mountain but that he went up *to God*? This is because revelations of God in the Bible most often took place on mountains. This interpretation is confirmed by what comes next: "The LORD called to him out of the mountain" (19:3). Then in his first words to Israel, YHWH conveyed something glorious. We should pay attention to the entire cluster of verses:

> You yourselves have seen what I did to the Egyptians, and how I bore you on eagles' wings and brought you to myself. Now therefore, if you will indeed obey my voice and keep my covenant, you shall be my treasured possession among all peoples, for all the earth is mine; and you shall be to me a kingdom of priests and a holy nation. (19:4–6)

The significance of this short passage can hardly be overstated. We recall that the events of this passage occurred after the exodus from Egypt and immediately before the revelation of God's instruction, his *torah*, to his people. And prior to those Ten Words of instruction, this word was filled with grace.

The first line of Exodus 19:4–6 offers a summary of the exodus from Egypt: YHWH defeated the Egyptians, YHWH bore Israel on eagles' wings, and YHWH brought Israel *to himself*. Even before Israel occupied the land of Canaan, the story of which is told in the book of Joshua, the return to Eden had begun. Whereas they had been expelled from YHWH's presence in YHWH's place, they had now been brought by YHWH *to himself*.

The next word of Exodus 19:4–6 is a call to obey: "If you will indeed obey my voice and keep my covenant . . ." This kind of language will make sense to those casually familiar with YHWH's covenant with Moses; staying in covenant blessing depended on Israel keeping the covenant. However, we must notice the context of this call to obedience: YHWH had just defeated the Egyptians, borne Israel on eagles' wings, and brought Israel to himself. This means that the order is important: Israel had already *become* the special people of YHWH in the covenant with Abraham (Gen. 15), and YHWH had acted on this covenant commitment in the exodus from Egypt. Now that Israel *had become* YHWH's special people, they were being called to *keep* the covenant this same YHWH was initiating with Moses and Israel.

This calls to mind a type of covenant common to Israel and her neighbors. In suzerain-vassal treaties, a powerful party (the suzerain) and a weaker party (the vassal) defined their relationship. Since the weaker vassal was completely dependent on the stronger suzerain for survival, it was appropriate for the stronger suzerain to set the terms of their relationship and to formalize it in a covenant. According to Exodus 19–24, YHWH, the ultimate suzerain who had just redeemed Israel out of slavery in Egypt, set the terms for his relationship with Israel, the dependent vassal who had just been rescued, and formalized it in a covenant. (While this covenant is most often referred to as YHWH's covenant with Moses, I have been referring to it as his covenant with Moses/Israel, because it can equally be called his covenant with Israel as a whole.)

Finally, Exodus 19:4–6 concludes with the blessings that would come from Israel's covenant-keeping: "You shall be my treasured possession among all peoples, for all the earth is mine; and you shall be to me a kingdom of priests and a holy nation." We can notice how the call to covenant-keeping in this passage is surrounded by grace, beforehand and now afterward. If Israel would keep the covenant that YHWH was making with them, they would be his treasured possession among all peoples; as Creator, all the earth was YHWH's possession, and he would set his favor on Israel.

And Israel would be to YHWH a kingdom of priests. What was the essence of a priest's role? Later in the book of Leviticus we learn of YHWH's institution of the priesthood, where a special group of Israelites would be set apart to mediate between YHWH and his people. But according to this passage in Exodus 19, Israel would also be an entire *kingdom* of priests. How would the blessings to the nations (as promised to Abraham) come to pass? It would be through Israel, as a kingdom of priests, who would mediate between YHWH and those nations. On the flip side, no one had more direct access to YHWH than a priest. Therefore, in Exodus 19:6 YHWH was also saying that Israel would be an entire kingdom of people who had special access to YHWH himself. Finally, Israel would be a holy people—a people consecrated for YHWH's presence.

As we look closely at Exodus 19:4–6, it is important to correct any misconceptions about a legalistic covenant between YHWH and Moses/Israel. Far from being based on works, it was clearly grace filled, even as it demanded the people's entire allegiance. In this way, it resembled the structure of the gospel demands in the New Testament:

> For by grace you have been saved through faith. And this is not your own doing; it is the gift of God, not a result of works, so that no one may boast. For we are his workmanship, created in Christ Jesus for good works, which God prepared beforehand, that we should walk in them. (Eph. 2:8–10)

In both the Old and New Testaments, grace precedes, but is also inseparably joined to, a call for complete, life-transforming allegiance.

After this awesome scene, Moses descended the mountain, called the elders of Israel, and conveyed these things to them (Ex. 19:7). And they responded by committing to do all that YHWH had spoken (19:8). The chapter closes by establishing a boundary for the people of Israel: they had to stay behind limits set by YHWH; since YHWH was about to descend in a thick cloud to the top of the mountain, the people could not even touch the mountain itself. The scene that followed was awesome:

> On the morning of the third day there were thunders and lightnings and a thick cloud on the mountain and a very loud trumpet blast, so that all the people in the camp trembled. Then Moses brought the people out of the camp to meet God, and they took their stand at the foot of the mountain. Now Mount Sinai was wrapped in smoke because the LORD had descended on it in fire. The smoke of it went up like the smoke of a kiln, and the whole mountain trembled greatly. And as the sound of the trumpet

grew louder and louder, Moses spoke, and God answered him in thunder. The LORD came down on Mount Sinai, to the top of the mountain. And the LORD called Moses to the top of the mountain, and Moses went up. (19:16–20)

After warning the people not to breach the limits set for them at the foot of the mountain, YHWH would then reveal more of his specific instructions for how to live as his special, redeemed people. Those words are recorded in Exodus 20.

Grace and Instruction in the Ten Words

As we come to Exodus 20, we encounter what most people know as the Ten Commandments. However, a closer look reveals that they are more accurately called the Ten Words (20:1).[3] These seventeen verses fill out the covenant obligation of Israel from Exodus 19:4–6, but once again they begin with grace: "I am the LORD your God, who brought you out of the land of Egypt, out of the house of slavery" (20:2). Before YHWH called Israel to any sort of behavior, he reminded them of what he had done for them. Grace always precedes instruction on how to live as YHWH's people. Put another way, in the Bible, good news of redemption always precedes instruction on how to live—whether speaking to old-covenant Israel or to new-covenant believers in Jesus.

Although there is some debate about how to count the Ten Words, for the sake of this study we will follow the most common Protestant understanding, as it is reflected in most English Bible

---

3 In Ex. 20:1 they are called "all these words." Then in Ex. 34:28; Deut. 4:13; 10:4 they are called the "Ten Words" in Hebrew, though the ESV translates this phrase as "Ten Commandments." However, in the New Testament they are explicitly referred to as "commandments" by Jesus (see Mark 10:19; Luke 18:20) and Paul (see Rom. 13:9; Eph. 6:2).

translations.[4] By that reckoning, the first three "words" had to do with Israel's relating to YHWH, the next one detailed the Sabbath as the sign of the covenant, and the last six had to do with Israel's relating to one another. The overall message of these Ten Words was clear: you have been redeemed, now live as the redeemed!

In light of what we have just learned, it is much easier to make sense of the Ten Words. The first literally instructed Israel not to have any other gods before YHWH's face (20:3). The second prohibited making an idol for worship (20:4–6). Finally, the third is most commonly translated, "You shall not take the name of the LORD your God in vain" (20:7). However, Carmen Imes points out that the Hebrew literally reads, "You must not *bear* [or *carry*] the name of Yahweh, your God, in vain, for Yahweh will not hold guiltless one who *bears* [or *carries*] his name in vain."[5] Did you notice the translation difference? While most English translations read "You shall not *take* the name of the LORD your God in vain," Imes suggests that a better translation has to do with *bearing* YHWH's name.

Imes then reflects on the way this same verb is used in Exodus 28 and its description of the high priest's ceremonial clothing:

His most striking item of clothing is his elaborate apron, woven with gold threads and set with twelve precious stones, each engraved like a seal with the name of one of the twelve tribes. And Moses is told that the high priest is to "*bear* (or *carry*) the names of the sons of Israel" as he moves in and out of the tabernacle

---

4 For a helpful discussion of this issue, along with a fresh proposal, see Carmen Joy Imes, *Bearing God's Name: Why Sinai Still Matters* (Downers Grove, IL: IVP Academic, 2019), 45–57.

5 Imes, *Bearing God's Name*, 49.

(Exodus 28:29). Moses' brother Aaron, who becomes Israel's first high priest, literally "carries" these tribal names whenever he is on duty.[6]

Imes notes further that since the high priest also wore the name YHWH on his forehead, along with the twelve stones on his breast-plate, the high priest represented the entire nation (made up of twelve tribes) before YHWH. Conversely, the YHWH medallion on his forehead indicated that he also represented YHWH to the nation.

Finally, Imes links all of this to Exodus 19, with Israel as YHWH's treasured possession, kingdom of priests, and holy nation: "As his treasured possession, Israel's vocation—the thing they were born to do—is to represent their God to the rest of humanity. They function in priestly ways, mediating between YHWH and everyone else."[7] In other words, just as the high priest represented Yahweh to the nation of Israel in Exodus 28:29, so in Exodus 20:7 Israel bore the name of YHWH before the nations—they represented YHWH to the nations.[8] In short, to bear YHWH's name in vain "would be to enter into this cove-nant relationship with him but to live no differently than the surrounding nations."[9] Daniel I. Block adds further that "to bear the name of God [also] means to have His name branded on one's person as a mark of divine ownership."[10] This adds the notion of *belonging* to the insights Imes has already offered.

---

6 Imes, *Bearing God's Name*, 49–50.
7 Imes, *Bearing God's Name*, 51.
8 See Imes, *Bearing God's Name*, 51.
9 Imes, *Bearing God's Name*, 53.
10 Daniel I. Block, *How I Love Your Torah, O Lord! Studies in the Book of Deuteronomy* (Eugene, OR: Wipf & Stock, 2011), 64, cited in Peter J. Gentry and Stephen J. Wellum, *Kingdom*

The next command is to keep the Sabbath, and Exodus 31:13 refers to this as the sign of YHWH's covenant with Moses/Israel. It was a participatory sign, reminding his people that he created the world in six days and then rested on the seventh. Since God's work of creation was complete, "the people were invited to enter his rest and enjoy his work."[11]

Finally, the last six commands had to do with the way the people of YHWH would relate to one another—they would be different from the surrounding nations. As a kingdom of priests and a holy nation who bore the name of YHWH before the nations and to each other, they would honor their father and mother; they would not murder or commit adultery or steal or bear false witness or covet (20:12–17). They were consecrated for YHWH, and they represented YHWH to the nations; whether then or now, God's people were/are called to a higher standard.

Grace and Instruction in the Case Laws

After the Ten Words of Exodus 20, we find a series of instructions for specific situations in Exodus 21–23. These are often called "case laws" because they dealt with specific situations. While the Ten Words offered a good summary of how Israel would live as the redeemed people of YHWH, the case laws—what are called "rules" or "judgments" in Exodus 21:1—got more specific. For example, in Exodus 21:16 YHWH instructed, "Whoever steals a man and sells him, and anyone found in possession of him, shall be put to death." Thus, the practice of kidnapping and selling victims into slavery was prohibited.

---

through Covenant: A Biblical-Theological Understanding of the Covenants, 2nd ed. (Wheaton, IL: Crossway, 2018), 377.

11 Gentry and Wellum, Kingdom through Covenant, 382.

Although we do not have the space to walk through each of these laws in detail, we do have space for a few principles that will help us to read them on our own. First, as we read the case laws it is important to remember that they were given in the flow of the larger Old Testament story. On its own, the instruction against kidnapping people and selling them into slavery may intuitively resonate with us as twenty-first-century Bible readers. But when we read this verse in light of YHWH's creation of men and women in his image and likeness, we can see just how evil such an act would be.

Second, there was implicitly grace in these case laws. It was a blessing that YHWH helped to unpack the general instruction of the Ten Words and showed how these applied to the nitty-gritty of Israel's life. Since they were the redeemed people of YHWH, the case laws clarified specifically how their lives would be different. When parents of young kids take their family bowling, they can arrange for gutter guards so that their kids will always knock some pins down. In a similar way that gutter guards guide a bowling ball toward the pins, the case laws were given as a means of grace to guide Israel in their daily lives; the life of the community would be better because they had this positive instruction.

Third, and finally, there is tension in the case laws. Perhaps some of us who are parents have experienced moments of exasperation when we looked at our kids and said, "I can't believe I have to tell you that what you just did was wrong." If, even after the flood, the intention of people's hearts has been evil from their youth (Gen. 8:21), wrong will inevitably sometimes feel right. And it is a shame that God's people needed to be told. But there is also tension for another reason: every single law that instructed Israel what to do "in the case" of a gross sin in the community was a reminder that they had not yet arrived at their ultimate destination. They had experienced the exodus from Egypt, they had been solidified as a great nation, and they would soon be settled in the promised land, but a full return to Eden was still beyond these blessings. Since sin was still going to be a part of the daily life of the community, and since *they had to be told* that stealing other human beings and selling them into slavery was wrong, the occupation of Canaan would not represent the *full* return to a new and better Eden that is the ultimate subject of the Bible's larger story.

From a New Testament perspective, we can relate: local churches and Christian families are communities of redeemed sinners. Although in the new covenant, YHWH transforms his people from the inside out, this happens progressively, which means we will inevitably sin against one another. In the Old Testament the ultimate destination was never the promised land, and in the New Testament the ultimate destination is not life in the local church. The instruction on what to do when gross sin happens among God's people reminds us that until the new heavens and the new earth, we have still not arrived at our ultimate destination.

The Golden Calf and the Compassion of YHWH

Although many other features of the book of Exodus remind us that Israel had not arrived at their ultimate destination, one more sticks out in particular. Exodus 32 records a scene from Israel's camp at the bottom of the mountain while Moses and the elders were up on Mount Sinai receiving the *torah* of YHWH. Prompted by Moses's long absence, the people came to Aaron and said, "Up, make us gods who shall go before us. As for this Moses, the man who brought us up out of the land of Egypt, we do not know what has become of him" (32:1). So Aaron took the lead: he gathered gold jewelry from the people, fashioned it with a graving tool, and made a golden calf (32:2–4). And the people responded, "These are your gods, O Israel, who brought you up out of the land of Egypt!" (32:4). Aaron built an altar before this image, and then declared that the next day would be a feast to YHWH (32:5). This meant that by worshiping the image of the golden calf, the community of God's people believed they would be worshiping YHWH himself.

The community followed through on these festivities, and YHWH responded by telling Moses to go down to the people who had corrupted themselves (32:6–8). In YHWH's estimation, the people were stubborn, and his wrath would burn against them to consume them. The scene that followed was awe-inspiring: Moses interceded for Israel in prayer and appealed to YHWH's reputation in the process. Specifically he prayed, "Why should the Egyptians say, 'With evil intent did he bring them out, to kill them in the mountains and to consume them from the face of the earth'?" (32:12). He also called on YHWH to remember Abraham, Isaac, and Israel and the covenant promises he had made to them (32:13). And so YHWH relented. Evidently, YHWH's reputation as the glorious Redeemer and YHWH's commitment to his covenant—his guarantee of redemption—were grounds for him to extend mercy to a people who deserved obliteration.

As Moses and Joshua descended Mount Sinai, they witnessed the scene, and Moses broke the tablets of YHWH's instruction; if Israel would break YHWH's instruction with their actions, Moses would show this symbolically by breaking the tablets on which that instruction was written (32:15–19). Moses also burned the golden calf, ground it to powder, scattered it on water, and made the people of Israel drink it (32:20). Next, when Moses called Aaron to account for his leadership, he blamed the people, and he also resorted to the ridiculous. Although Exodus 32:4 makes clear that

Aaron had *fashioned* the calf with a graving tool, he summarized, "I said to them, 'Let any who have gold take it off.' So they gave it to me, and I threw it into the fire, and *out came this calf*" (32:24).

The scene that followed was a bloody reminder of the wages of sin: Moses had the people of Levi kill three thousand of the offenders with swords (32:26–29). But this was not enough. Moses then ascended the mountain again to seek *atonement*, or forgiveness, for the sins of the people. He offered to be blotted out from YHWH's book if the people would not be forgiven, but YHWH responded by saying he would only blot out the sinners themselves (32:32–33). So YHWH sent a plague among the people because of the calf that Aaron had made (32:35).

As we look back on Exodus 32, what do we learn? First, we learn that it is not enough to intend to worship YHWH; we must worship him *in the way he prescribes*. Although the people believed that worshiping YHWH through the image of a calf was a good thing, it was not. Next, we learn that sin is deadly serious before a holy God. In fact, in this scene it resulted in immediate death for three thousand people. But this was simply a temporal reminder of the eternal consequences of sin.

As the passage continues, we encounter something glorious in the midst of the bleakness. To summarize Exodus 33, YHWH told Moses to lead the people into the promised land but that he would not go with his sinful nation. However, Moses refused because the main point of the promised land was to have YHWH dwelling in their midst. Milk and honey (i.e., abundance) would not be wonderful without the presence of their covenant God. YHWH agreed to go with them, and then Moses asked for something audacious: he asked YHWH to show him his glory. YHWH agreed: "I will make all my goodness pass before you and will proclaim before you my name 'The LORD.' And I will be gracious to whom I will be gracious, and will show mercy on whom I will show mercy" (33:19). But Moses could not see YHWH's face and live, so YHWH put him in a cleft of a rock and covered him with his hand until he passed by. Then YHWH removed his hand so that Moses could see his back. We read:

> The LORD passed before him and proclaimed, "The LORD, the LORD, a God merciful and gracious, slow to anger, and abounding in steadfast love and faithfulness, keeping steadfast love for thousands, forgiving iniquity and transgression and sin, but who will by no means clear the guilty, visiting the iniquity of the fathers on the children and the children's children, to the third and the fourth generation." (34:6–7)

We see this summary of YHWH's character repeated throughout the Old Testament—especially in the Minor Prophets. In response to this glorious scene, Moses asked YHWH to go with Israel into the promised land, and YHWH agreed—the merciful, gracious, slow to anger one, who abounded in steadfast love and faithfulness, showed his glorious character to his rebellious, idolatrous people.

Looking Forward to Christ: The Faithful Son of God and the New and Better Lawgiver

In Matthew, Mark, and Luke, the account of Jesus's baptism is immediately followed by his temptation in the wilderness. In the baptism of Jesus, the sinless Son of God identified with sinners—especially sinful Israel. The Spirit of God also descended like a dove onto him, and a voice from heaven said, "This is my beloved Son, with whom I am well pleased" (Matt. 3:17). Immediately afterward, "Jesus was led up by the Spirit into the wilderness to be tempted by the devil" (Matt. 4:1). It is significant that Jesus had been clearly identified as the beloved Son of God *before* his temptation—it was not just anyone who would enter into this intense period of temptation, but the beloved Son of God, the Lord Jesus.

Then in his temptation, Jesus continued to identify with sinful Israel. But whereas Israel wandered in the wilderness for forty years, Jesus was led by the Spirit into the wilderness and fasted for forty days and forty nights. Whereas Israel broke YHWH's grace-filled covenant, Jesus—the ultimate faithful Israelite—was tested and found faithful. Theologians refer to this as the active obedience of Christ—he actively obeyed where we (and Israel and every person in history) have failed. He could later be the perfect sacrifice for our sins because he was tested and found faithful, the beloved Son of God. For this reason we can be forgiven—because Jesus lived the perfect life that we failed to live, and he died the death that we deserved to die.[12]

Earlier in this chapter we noticed that the Bible most often records revelations of God on mountains; when his leaders specially encountered him and received instruction by him, this was where the action happened. For this reason, it is significant that Jesus preached his longest recorded sermon "on the *mountain*" (Matt. 5:1). When we as Christians first encounter this sermon, its place of delivery most often gets a footnote in our thinking; we think it is interesting, but we assume that it does not have any bearing on the sermon's significance. However, when we read the Sermon on the Mount in the context of the whole Bible, we can see clearly that just as Moses went up a mountain to meet with God and

---

12 I first heard this wonderful gospel summary in the ministry of Timothy Keller.

receive his instruction for the people, so Jesus's disciples went up a mountain to receive instruction from Jesus (who is God the Son) for the new-covenant community of God's people. And as we have seen, this came *after* his baptism and *after* he was found faithful in his test with the devil.

In a previous chapter we saw that in the new covenant, the instruction of YHWH would be written on his people's hearts (Jer. 31:31–34; Ezek. 36:26–27). In this context, we can better understand the Sermon on the Mount. Far from abolishing the Old Testament *Torah* or the Prophets, Jesus had come to fulfill them (Matt. 5:17). According to Jesus's teaching, not even the smallest point would pass away from YHWH's Old Testament instruction until all was accomplished. And then it got intense: with a series of "You have heard that it was said . . . , but I say to you" statements, Jesus intensified the Old Testament instruction. For the new-covenant people of God—who would be given the Holy Spirit and be able to obey from the heart—the standard was not lower but higher than the word of YHWH to Moses.

To sum up these glorious truths, the one who came to save his people from their sins (Matt. 1:21) was also the beloved Son of God, tested and faithful. *And* he was the new and better lawgiver, whose word called his people to a higher standard even as the Holy Spirit was given to enable this radical obedience from the heart. Just as YHWH redeemed Israel *before* he instructed them how to live as his people, so Jesus offers free forgiveness of sins and also instruction about how his followers must live.

Discussion Questions

1. The author argued that Sinai is central to the story of the Pentateuch. Restate his argument and share if you think it has merit.

2. What does the Hebrew word *torah* mean? How does this meaning contribute to viewing YHWH's covenant with Moses more positively and less legalistically?

3. The author argued that grace is consistently the context of YHWH's calls to obedience in Exodus 19–24. What are some of the key points he made about grace in these chapters? Did you find his argument convincing or wanting?

4. What does it mean that Israel would be a "kingdom of priests"?

5. Recall Carmen Imes's insight about bearing the name of YHWH in vain (Ex. 20:7) and its relationship with the high priest's wardrobe in Exodus 28:29. How does her insight help us to better apply this command to our twenty-first-century lives?

6. The author listed some key lessons from the scene of the golden calf in Exodus 32. Did any of these stick out to you as particularly relevant for our day? Explain why you think this is the case.

7. What are some key insights we can learn from Jesus's baptism, his temptation, and his Sermon on the Mount?

7

Tabernacle, Priesthood, and Sacrifice

Provisions for the Redeemed

CAN A LONG SET OF INSTRUCTIONS about an ancient tent dwelling for Israel's God have *any* relevance to our twenty-first-century lives? And the same could be asked about priests who offered bloody sacrifices. We don't worship in this type of structure anymore, nor do we find priests and a lineup of condemned animals on our way into church for Sunday worship.

As many readers encounter the book of Exodus, they experience the first half as monumental and edifying and the second half as boring and benign. Apart from isolated passages, the latter fifteen chapters may feel out of sync with our twenty-first-century lives. The same trajectory continues through the entire next book, as Leviticus seems even further out of sync and even less interesting.

Although this is the initial experience of many, we should remember that God included these portions of his word for a reason. As we learn why they are in the Bible, and as we learn what they communicate, we are better equipped to experience their riches. In fact, the stories of the construction of the tabernacle and the instructions about the priesthood in the latter half of Exodus, along with the beginning of the functioning priesthood and the sacrificial system in the book of Leviticus, were all given as precious provisions for those YHWH had redeemed from slavery in Egypt.[1] Although these symbols are not in use today—because Jesus has fulfilled them—we are better equipped to understand the person and work of Jesus as we first understand the Pentateuch's teaching on them.

Tabernacle

The main focus of Exodus 25–40 is on the construction of the tabernacle.[2] Since YHWH gave Israel favor with the Egyptians on their way out, they had gold and jewels and fabrics on hand (12:35–36; cf. 3:21–22). In Exodus 25 YHWH commissioned Moses to ask

1 My approach to this material has been especially shaped by L. Michael Morales, *Who Shall Ascend the Mountain of the Lord? A Biblical Theology of the Book of Leviticus*, New Studies in Biblical Theology 37, ed. D. A. Carson (Downers Grove, IL: InterVarsity Press, 2015). In addition, John Mahaffey, who is the lead pastor of our family's church in Hamilton, Ontario, preached very helpful messages on the latter portion of Exodus in the spring of 2021, and these helped to shape my thinking further. See John Mahaffey, "The Gospel according to Exodus," sermon series (2021), West Highland Baptist Church, Ontario, Canada, https://www.westhighland.org/. Mahaffey lists three books as most formative in his own thinking on the book of Exodus. Since preachers do not add footnotes to their sermons, I list these books in this place in order to give them their due credit for their influence on Mahaffey's preaching and therefore my thinking: Philip Graham Ryken, *Exodus: Saved for God's Glory*, Preaching the Word (Wheaton, IL: Crossway, 2005); Tim Chester, *Exodus for You* (Surrey, UK: Good Book Company, 2016); J. A. Motyer, *The Message of Exodus* (Downers Grove, IL: IVP Academic, 2005).

2 More precisely, in Ex. 25–27, 30, YHWH gave instructions for building the tabernacle and its utensils, and in Ex. 35–38 those instructions were carried out in their construction. Finally, in Ex. 40 the tabernacle was erected. Although many sources have helped my understanding of the tabernacle over the years, I was especially helped more recently by the following sermon: John Mahaffey, "There Is No Place Like Home: Exodus 25–27, Hebrews 9:1–14," May 2, 2021, West Highland Baptist Church, Hamilton, Ontario, Canada, https://www.westhighland.org/.

for contributions for the divine dwelling place. Although this may not seem exciting to us, think about what it meant in the flow of the Bible: although YHWH's special presence with his people had been lost after the fall into sin, the construction of the tabernacle would initiate a "return to Eden," because for the first time since the garden paradise, YHWH would dwell in their midst. As Morales put it, "The first half of Exodus restores a knowledge of Yahweh to the world through the exodus (Exodus 1–15), and the second half restores the presence of Yahweh to humanity through the covenant gift of his tabernacling presence to Israel (Exodus 16–40)."[3]

Let's imagine that we have been given VIP access to a virtual tour of this ancient tabernacle. As we take our tour with Scripture-filled minds, we quickly notice that the tabernacle was meant to point beyond itself to spiritual realities. From the very beginning of our tour, when we enter the structure on the east, our minds are immediately drawn to the exit out of Eden:

> Then the LORD God said, "Behold, the man has become like one of us in knowing good and evil. Now, lest he reach out his hand and take also of the tree of life and eat, and live forever—" therefore the LORD God sent him out from the garden of Eden to work the ground from which he was taken. He drove out the man, and *at the east of the garden of Eden he placed the cherubim and a flaming sword that turned every way to guard the way to the tree of life.* (Gen. 3:22–24)

As we learn to be careful readers of the Bible, we notice that its details are rarely incidental. In this case, since the exit out of Eden

---

3 L. Michael Morales, *Exodus Old and New*, Essential Studies in Biblical Theology 2, ed. Benjamin L. Gladd (Downers Grove, IL: IVP Academic, 2020), 39.

was on the east, the placement of the entrance to the tabernacle on the east signals the beginnings of a return to Eden, and more specifically, a return to the presence of YHWH. In the flow of the Bible we can say that the tabernacle was a monumental first step toward the ultimate goal of redemption: God's people dwelling unhindered in his presence for eternity. Although this will ultimately be fulfilled in a new heaven and a new earth (Rev. 21:1), the tabernacle of Exodus signaled a step toward this awesome goal. Through its entrance on the east, Israel was invited to reenter the presence of God that had been lost since the fall into sin.

As we continue our virtual tour of the ancient tabernacle, we discover that worshipers who entered on the east would find themselves in a fenced-in courtyard. This was a fairly open space, and it contained a bronze altar and a bronze basin, indicating the need for blood atonement and cleansing in order to enter the presence of YHWH.

Before we move beyond the courtyard, a drone shot lifts our gaze to view the whole structure from above. This reveals three zones: the courtyard and then a tent that contained the Holy Place and the Most Holy Place. Each of these zones hearkens our minds back to the three zones of Mount Sinai, where Moses received the *torah* from YHWH. The courtyard of the tabernacle corresponds to the bottom of the mountain where the people camped, the Holy Place corresponds to the point on the mountain where YHWH met with the elders of the people, and the Most Holy Place corresponds to the summit of the mountain, where Moses met with YHWH. As John Mahaffey put it, in this way "the tabernacle replicated and perpetuated the experience of Sinai."[4] Furthermore, the fabrics

---

4   John Mahaffey, "A Priest to Guide Us Home: Exodus 28–30," sermon, May 9, 2021, West Highland Baptist Church, Hamilton, Ontario, Canada, https://www.westhighland.org/. Mahaffey is echoing Chester, *Exodus for You*, 207.

and metals in each of these zones grew more precious from the courtyard to the Holy Place to the Most Holy Place. As another author points out, "The more precious the materials and the more intricate the workmanship involved, the more important the object, and therefore the greater the level of sanctity assigned to it."[5]

As we return to a "boots on the ground" view in our tour, we move beyond the courtyard, through the first curtain, and into zone two—the Holy Place. Here we find a table, a golden lampstand, twelve loaves of bread, and an altar of incense. On the table are the golden lampstand and the twelve loaves—called "the bread of the Presence." While the shape of the lampstand—as a tree—represented the tree of life, Morales adds that "the light of the lampstand represents the life-giving Presence of God, his blessed glory, while the twelve loaves represent the twelve tribes of Israel."[6] The lampstand was to have its light facing forward, so that it shone onto the bread of the Presence. Morales explains further that "*this arrangement portrayed visually God's intention that his people should live continually in his presence and enjoy the blessing mediated by priests.*"[7]

Finally, we reach the third zone through another curtain, but this curtain is embroidered with images of cherubim. If the entrance on the east reminded us of the exit out of Eden, the cherubim on this curtain recall the same scene, where cherubim and a flaming sword guarded the way to the tree of life (Gen. 3:24). This image on the curtain reminded the ancient worshiper that although YHWH was opening a way for his people to enter his presence, there was

---

5 W. Ross Blackburn, *The God Who Makes Himself Known: The Missionary Heart of the Book of Exodus*, New Studies in Biblical Theology 28, ed. D. A. Carson (Downers Grove, IL: InterVarsity Press, 2012), 127.

6 Morales, *Who Shall Ascend the Mountain of the Lord?*, 17.

7 Morales, *Who Shall Ascend the Mountain of the Lord?*, 16; emphasis original.

still a measure of separation between the redeemed and their Redeemer—cherubim still guarded the entrance to YHWH's presence.

This third zone was called the Most Holy Place, and it was the center of the entire structure. As we venture in, our eyes view a room that only the high priest could enter, and then only once per year. The centerpiece in this inner core was the ark of the covenant,[8] a wooden chest, overlaid with pure gold. Inside this box were the stone tablets of the Ten Words, along with some manna and Aaron's staff that budded (see Heb. 9:4). In keeping with ancient Near Eastern practice, the placement of the stone tablets of the covenant law into the ark symbolized that God was King and Israel was his subject.[9] On the bottom were two wooden poles overlaid with gold, and these were used for transport—human hands were not to touch the ark itself.

On top of the ark were two golden cherubim that faced each other but looked downward in reverent awe. As one author put it, "Because artists often used cherubim-like figures on throne pedestals, the cherubim atop the ark symbolize a throne; thus God is 'enthroned' above the cherubim (1 Sam 4:4; 2 Sam 6:2; 2 Kings 19:15; Ps 80:1; 99:1; Is 37:16; cf. Num 7:89; Ezek 9:3)."[10] This is stated explicitly in 1 Chronicles 13:6, which refers to "the ark of God, which is called by the name of the LORD who sits enthroned above the cherubim." Tim Chester explains more about what it meant for YHWH to sit enthroned *above* the cherubim: since the ark "has the same proportions as the footstool of an ancient king

---

8 My explanation of the ark of the covenant was especially helped by Kenneth Laing Harris, "The Ark of the Covenant," in *ESV Study Bible*, ed. Wayne Grudem (Wheaton, IL: Crossway, 2008), Accordance electronic ed., 2346.

9 See Chester, *Exodus for You*, 189.

10 "Tabernacle," in *Dictionary of Biblical Imagery*, ed. Leland Ryken, James C. Wihoit, and Tremper Longman III (Downers Grove, IL: InterVarsity Press, 1998), 838.

. . . the LORD is, as it were, seated on his throne in heaven with the ark as his footstool on earth."[11] These images combine to paint a picture of a community (Israel) that lived under YHWH's reign. These cherubim were stretched out over the mercy seat, and it was from between these cherubim that YHWH spoke to Moses, who represented the people of Israel (Ex. 25:22).

While we may have had a clear view of the ark during our virtual tour, Israel's high priest would not have seen so clearly. During his once-per-year entrance into this sacred space on the Day of Atonement, he carried incense that intentionally obscured his view:

> The high priest enters the dimly lit tabernacle with trepidation. In one hand is a censer, hot with glowing coals from the altar. In the other are two handfuls of incense. As he moves behind the curtain into the [Most Holy Place], he puts the incense on the coals, producing a fragrant cloud over the ark of the covenant, the footstool of Yahweh. Thus the place of the Presence is shrouded in aromatic smoke, and the priest is hindered from seeing the forbidden throne of God.[12]

This incense also symbolized something glorious: as its smoke filled the Most Holy Place, the imagery hearkened back to the cloudy summit of Mount Sinai, where Moses met with YHWH; as he entered this holy space, the high priest was encountering the very presence of YHWH.

Although this concludes our virtual tour, we can notice that two different terms were used for this one structure, and each emphasized

---

11 Chester, *Exodus for You*, 188.
12 "Incense," in *Dictionary of Biblical Imagery*, 418–19.

a different aspect of its purpose. On the one hand, the tabernacle was called "the dwelling place" of YHWH, the place where YHWH's glory could reside in the midst of a sin-cursed world. On the other hand, the tabernacle was also called "the tent of meeting" between YHWH and his people—specifically the priests among his people. It was not enough that YHWH's glory would dwell in a cube-shaped tent; a full return to Eden would mean that interaction, meeting between YHWH and his people, would be reestablished.

In light of what we have just learned, the scene at the end of Exodus takes on a new significance as the glory of YHWH filled the tabernacle. For the first time since the garden of Eden, Israel would live with YHWH dwelling in her midst. However, Morales points out that there was also a crisis in this scene, because Moses was not allowed to enter. At the end of Exodus, something *was* accomplished: the tabernacle had become "the dwelling place" of YHWH. However, something more needed to be accomplished; it was not yet a place where *any* of the people (including Moses) could meet with YHWH—it was not yet a "tent of meeting."[13] If the greatest prophet in Israel's history could not enter the presence of YHWH, how could Israel become a kingdom of priests to mediate YHWH's presence to the surrounding nations (Ex. 19:6)? For that to happen, they needed the book of Leviticus and its teaching about the priesthood and the sacrificial system. Only with these could the way into YHWH's presence be opened.

Priesthood

The beginning of a functioning priesthood represented the first step toward resolving the crisis at the end of the book of Exodus—

---

13 See Morales, *Who Shall Ascend the Mountain of the Lord?*, 110.

without this step, humanity would not be able to enter YHWH's presence. As a way of understanding the significance of this role, we will focus on the high priest and specifically some key features of his priestly clothing (see Exodus 28 and 39 for full instructions).

First, the high priest wore a long, sleeveless garment called an ephod. Its colors were chosen intentionally: "Blue and purple were the most expensive colors available and were associated with royalty and power, while scarlet was associated with blood and ritual cleansing."[14] This ephod was adorned with an onyx stone on each shoulder, and these were engraved with the names of the twelve tribes of Israel—six on each stone. On the one hand, this reminds us of the garden of Eden once again—remember that onyx stones were found there (Gen. 2:12). On the other hand, the symbol was of the high priest bearing the twelve tribes of Israel on his shoulders wherever he went (see Ex. 28:6–12).

Next, the high priest's breastpiece had twelve gemstones woven into its fabric, many of which also appeared in the garden of Eden. These will also come into view later in the biblical story, in the picture of the new Jerusalem (see Rev. 21). Each gemstone was engraved with a name of one of the twelve tribes of Israel. Together, the twelve gemstones symbolized the twelve tribes as YHWH's treasured possession (see Ex. 28:15–30). This breastpiece also contained a pouch containing the Urim and the Thummim: "As mediator between God and Israel, the high priest could inquire of God by the Urim and Thummim and so maintain Israel's rights and privileges with God."[15] In summary, as the high priest entered the tabernacle, the twelve tribes were not only borne on his shoulders (engraved

---

14 C. Van Dam, "Priestly Clothing" in *Dictionary of the Old Testament: Pentateuch*, ed. T. Desmond Alexander and David W. Baker (Downers Grove, IL: IVP Academic, 2003), 643.

15 Van Dam, "Priestly Clothing," 644.

on the onyx stones), but they were also front and center on his chest (and over his heart). In this way, he symbolically carried the community into the presence of YHWH (28:12, 29).

The high priest also wore a seamless robe with small pomegranates, which signified abundance, Eden. The robe also had bells, and these served a more sobering purpose: if the high priest died in the glorious presence of YHWH, the bells would stop ringing and the community would be made aware of his death. He also wore a turban with a gold plate on his forehead that read, "Holy to the LORD" (28:36). Even his underwear was significant; in Exodus 28:42–43 we learn that it went from waist to thigh. Unlike the pagan priests of Israel's neighbors, YHWH's priest entered the tabernacle with modesty. So the clothing of the high priest was symbol laden. In addition to the things we have already mentioned, the clothing was meant to give a sense of the sacred, of the majesty of God.

To summarize, the priests in general and the high priest in particular were mediators between YHWH and his people. If the ultimate goal was for Israel to be a kingdom of priests (19:6), they first needed their own priests to mediate between YHWH and their community. The way back to the presence of YHWH was beginning, but this needed one more essential piece: the sacrificial system.

Sacrifice

In the previous chapter, we noticed that Sinai is central to the story of the Pentateuch. Since sixty-eight chapters precede the arrival of Israel at the wilderness of Sinai, sixty chapters follow their departure, and fifty-nine chapters tell the story of their stay at Sinai, one way we can split up the story of the Pentateuch is into these three parts. But as we continue to look closely at the material, a bit more math reveals something startling: of the fifty-nine chapters that tell the story of Israel at Sinai, twenty-seven come before the institution of the Day of Atonement, and twenty-one after. This means that, roughly speaking, Leviticus 16 and the story of the Day of Atonement are at the center of the center of the Pentateuch's story.[16] Because of its centrality, in this section we'll unpack what this Day of Atonement entailed.

As we begin with the big picture, Morales observes that the general topic of Leviticus 1–15 is approaching God through atonement, and the general topic of Leviticus 17–27 is communion with God through holiness; at the center is Leviticus 16 with its theme of cleansing.[17] This observation suggests that the Day of Atonement was the capstone of the sacrificial rituals of the first part of Leviticus and flowed out into the subject of holy living after this important chapter.[18]

Leading up to the Day of Atonement of Leviticus 16, numerous sacrificial offerings are detailed in Leviticus 1–15. As we remember the ultimate goal—that YHWH's people would draw near to him—Leviticus emphasizes that Israel's sins must first be dealt with. As Morales put it, "Only a cleansed humanity may belong to YHWH. The way to God, then, is through a bloody knife and a burning altar."[19] The animals for these sacrifices needed to be without blemish (e.g., Lev. 1:3).[20] This way, the worshiper experienced great personal cost, and the offering also suggested the idea

---

16 I first learned this from Morales, *Who Shall Ascend the Mountain of the Lord?*, 167. More precisely, in this place Morales refers to the Day of Atonement as "the structural and thematic centre of the Pentateuch, the literary summit to which and from which the narrative drama ascends and descends."

17 See Morales, *Who Shall Ascend the Mountain of the Lord?*, 29.

18 See Morales, *Who Shall Ascend the Mountain of the Lord?*, 29.

19 Morales, *Who Shall Ascend the Mountain of the Lord?*, 124.

20 Although a more thorough discussion of the distinctions between clean and unclean, holy and profane, is beyond the scope of this book, interested readers can see especially Morales,

of the animal dying in place of the sinful worshiper.[21] This "worked" because an animal that was without blemish "served to symbolize the morally blameless life, a life of whole-hearted submission to the will of God."[22] And as worshipers laid their hands on the spotless animal's head, the animal became a blameless substitute for them as its blood was poured out in their place.

This brings us to Leviticus 16 and the Day of Atonement. On this holy day, Aaron the priest was to bathe his body, get dressed in his priestly clothing, and take two male goats for a sin offering and one ram for a burnt offering (Lev. 16:3–5). He was to offer a bull as a sin offering for himself and his house; before Aaron could approach YHWH, blood atonement needed to be made for his sin (16:6). Put another way, if this sin-stained son of Adam was going to approach YHWH on behalf of the people, he would need to be cleansed and then covered by the death of something innocent.

Next, Aaron was to take the two goats to the entrance of the tent of meeting and cast lots over them. The goat whose lot fell on YHWH was to be used as a sin offering, and the goat whose lot fell on Azazel was to be "presented alive before the LORD to make atonement over it, that it may be sent away into the wilderness to Azazel" (Lev. 16:10).[23] Morales explains that "the goats, as one symbol, stand for the sake of Israel: the sacrificed goat conveying Israel favourably into the inner sanctum vicari-

---

Who Shall Ascend the Mountain of the Lord?, 153–67; Matthew Thiessen, Jesus and the Forces of Death (Grand Rapids, MI: Baker Academic, 2020), 9–14.

21 See Morales, Who Shall Ascend the Mountain of the Lord?, 125.

22 Morales, Who Shall Ascend the Mountain of the Lord?, 127.

23 The meaning of the term "Azazel" is debated. For a helpful discussion of various positions, see especially J. E. Hartley, "Day of Atonement," in Dictionary of the Old Testament: Pentateuch, 59.

ously, the led-away goat conveying Israel's sins away from the face of God."[24]

Aaron (the first high priest) was to then fill the Most Holy Place with "the cloud of incense" and sprinkle some blood from the bull and the goat on the mercy seat (16:12–16). As we have seen, while the cloud recalled Moses's approach to YHWH at the summit of Mount Sinai, it also protected Aaron by shielding his eyes from the glory of YHWH. And the blood once again symbolized atonement for sin, this time for the people as a whole. Outside the Holy Place, blood was again to be sprinkled on the horns of the altar, to "cleanse it and consecrate it from the uncleannesses of the people of Israel" (Lev. 16:19).

With the blood-cleansing complete, Aaron was to lay his hands on the head of the live goat, confess over it the iniquities, transgressions, and sins of the people of Israel, and then send it away into the wilderness (16:20–22). In this way, "the goat shall bear all their iniquities on itself to a remote area . . . in the wilderness" (16:22). After another bath for Aaron—more cleansing!—he was to offer a burnt offering for himself and one for the people as well, to make atonement for all (16:23–25). Then the remains of the sacrificed animals were to be burned outside the camp. Finally, even the one who burned the animals needed to bathe before reentering the camp (16:27–28).

The overall purpose of this solemn ceremony was then given: "For on this day shall atonement be made for you to cleanse you. You shall be clean before the LORD from all your sins" (16:30). The chapter then closes with a note about the duration of this ceremony: "And this shall be a statute forever for you,

24 Morales, *Who Shall Ascend the Mountain of the Lord?*, 180.

that atonement may be made for the people of Israel *once in the year* because of all their sins" (16:34). Leviticus then concludes with details about other annual festivals—"a sure signal that the dwelling of God has indeed become the tent of meeting between Israel and God."[25]

Before we move on, we need to remind ourselves that the covenant between YHWH and Moses/Israel was the context for the sacrifices outlined in the book of Leviticus. Therefore, these sacrifices did not *earn* YHWH's favor so that Israel could *become* his people; they were given *to* his redeemed people as a gift, as provisions so that they could approach his presence and remain his people. Because YHWH's people were sinful, they could not approach him on their own. Because they were redeemed, they were given a tabernacle so that YHWH could dwell among them, a priesthood to intercede for them, and a sacrificial system so that an animal could die the death that they deserved to die.[26] Under YHWH's covenant with Moses/Israel, the tabernacle, priesthood, and sacrificial system were precious *provisions*, so that a sinful people could live with YHWH in their midst.

This great provision is on full display when we notice Moses's proximity to YHWH as the Pentateuch unfolds. If the book of Exodus had ended with Moses's inability to enter into the glory-filled tabernacle (also called a "tent of meeting," Ex. 40:35), and in the first verse of Leviticus YHWH spoke to Moses *from* the tent of meeting, in the first verse of Numbers YHWH spoke to Moses *in* the tent of meeting. In the first two scenes, Moses was outside the tent of meeting, and in the last, he was inside, in YHWH's presence. What accomplished this movement toward YHWH?

25 Morales, *Who Shall Ascend the Mountain of the Lord?*, 185.
26 I first heard this wonderful gospel summary in the ministry of Timothy Keller.

The book of Leviticus shows us that with the beginning of the functioning priesthood and the sacrificial system, mediators and blood atonement for sin allowed Moses to enter the presence of YHWH. Therefore, the tension at the end of the book of Exodus and the beginning of the book of Leviticus was resolved by the book of Leviticus. Morales summarizes beautifully: "If Genesis may be adequately labelled 'the longing for Eden,' and Exodus 'the return to Eden,' then Leviticus may similarly be subtitled 'entering the garden of Eden,' especially with reference to Leviticus 16 as its central chapter."[27] Because of this essential book of the Pentateuch, Moses could finally draw near into YHWH's presence.[28]

Looking Forward to Christ: The New and Better Tabernacle/Temple, the Great High Priest, and the Ultimate Sacrifice

As we turn to the New Testament, we find that Jesus is presented as the fulfillment of this entire system of tabernacle, priesthood, and sacrifice. In the prologue to John's Gospel, Jesus is said to be "the Word" who "became flesh" and literally "pitched his tent," or "tabernacled" among us (John 1:14). If the purpose of the tabernacle was to have YHWH dwelling in the midst of his people—an initial step toward a full return to Eden—Jesus was the true and better tabernacle, who is elsewhere called Immanuel, God with us (Isa. 7:14; Matt. 1:23).

In the next chapter of John's Gospel, the Jews asked Jesus for a sign to prove his claims, and he answered, "Destroy this temple, and in three days I will raise it up" (John 2:19). Although these Jews thought he was talking about the physical temple, John explained,

---

27 Morales, *Who Shall Ascend the Mountain of the Lord?*, 173.

28 I am thankful to my friend Andrew W. Hall for sharing the insight that YHWH spoke to Moses *from* the tent of meeting in Lev. 1:1 and *in* the tent of meeting in Num. 1:1.

"He was speaking about the temple of his body" (John 2:21). We know from 1 Kings that a permanent temple later replaced the tent structure of the tabernacle. According to the Gospel of John, Jesus not only "tabernacled" among us, but his body was also the temple. What do these things mean? If the tabernacle (and later the temple) brought the presence of YHWH into the community of God's people, in Jesus we find the fulfillment of this temporary Old Testament locale—in the person of Jesus the tabernacle/temple of God's presence had arrived. The physical temple was no longer needed because Jesus *was* the temple.

While the tabernacle/temple was the most powerful place to experience God's presence in the Old Testament, after the ascension of Jesus and the sending of the Holy Spirit in Acts 1–2, all who are "in Christ" are temples of the Holy Spirit (e.g., 1 Cor. 3:16; 6:19). Even more incredible is what is coming: the new Jerusalem that will come down out of heaven from God (Rev. 21:2). This will be a cube-shaped locale—a bigger and better garden of Eden and an enormous version of the Most Holy Place. But this city will have no temple, "for its temple is the Lord God the Almighty and the Lamb" (Rev. 21:22). And it will have no need of sun, moon, or stars because God will be its light and its lamp will be the Lamb (Rev. 22:5). From humanity's first banishment from God's presence in the garden of Eden to the tabernacle, to the temple, to Jesus, to the church, these are stops along the way that lead us to the ultimate hope of a new and better Eden: the new heavens and the new earth, where God will dwell among his people *forever.* Amen. Come, Lord Jesus!

Not only does the New Testament present Jesus as the fulfillment of the tabernacle/temple but also of the high priest. The author of Hebrews put it beautifully:

Since then we have a great high priest who has passed through the heavens, Jesus, the Son of God, let us hold fast our confession. For we do not have a high priest who is unable to sympathize with our weaknesses, but one who in every respect has been tempted as we are, yet without sin. Let us then with confidence draw near to the throne of grace, that we may receive mercy and find grace to help in time of need. (Heb. 4:14–16)

Notice that Jesus is not merely the *new* high priest, but rather, the *great* high priest. While the high priest of the Old Testament needed to atone for his own sins before he could atone for the sins of the people, Jesus was (and is) a sinless mediator (Heb. 5:3; 7:27). And while the Old Testament high priest was a human mediator, the God-man, Jesus Christ, passed through the heavens. Finally, while a divine high priest would be powerful, the incarnation and life of Jesus means that our great high priest can sympathize with our weaknesses, even as he invites us to boldly come to his throne of grace.

Finally, the reason Jesus could invite his people to come boldly to his throne of grace is that he was also the ultimate sacrifice for our sins. While the Old Testament instituted a complex and bloody sacrificial system as a provision to allow the redeemed to live as the people of YHWH, the author of Hebrews offered a shocking reflection: "It is *impossible* for the blood of bulls and goats to take away sins" (Heb. 10:4). This means that the Old Testament sacrifices were *prospective*—they looked forward to Christ. The reason Old Testament saints could be forgiven of their sins was that Jesus would come and be the ultimate sacrifice to which the Old Testament sacrificial system pointed. This is why there is no longer a need to sacrifice for sins today: the offering of Jesus was a once-for-all sacrifice (Heb. 10:10).

As we have reflected on the Old Testament tabernacle, priesthood, and sacrificial system, we have been saying that they were provisions for the redeemed. And their overall purpose was to open a way for humanity to reenter the presence of YHWH that was lost when Adam plunged us into sin. In the context of the Bible, however, the tabernacle, priesthood, and sacrificial system were *temporary* pointers toward the greater end, who is Christ. This helps to explain what happened when Jesus died on the cross: the Gospel writers tell us that the curtain of the temple was torn in two, from top to bottom (Matt. 27:51; Mark 15:38). What was the purpose of this curtain? The purpose was to separate the Most Holy Place, where YHWH dwelled, from sinful humanity. In fact, only the high priest could enter through this cherubim-embroidered curtain and into the Most Holy Place. And he could only do this once per year (on the Day of Atonement), and in a cloud of incense to shield his eyes from the glory of YHWH. But when Jesus died, this curtain was torn in two! And notice how it was torn: from top to bottom. In other words, it was torn by God. When Jesus died on the cross for our sins, our heavenly Father removed the cherubim-embroidered barrier that guarded the way to his presence. By the blood of Jesus, Christians are given access to YHWH's presence every day!

Discussion Questions

1. If you have read the latter portion of Exodus and the book of Leviticus in the past, did you find them difficult? If so, why?

2. As the host of a virtual tour, the author listed various items in the tabernacle along with its various zones. Share a few insights from this tour that you found particularly helpful.

3. The author listed various aspects of the high priest's wardrobe along with their symbolic purpose. Share a few that you found particularly helpful.

4. Along with Michael Morales, the author suggested that a single chapter in the Pentateuch is most central. Which chapter is he referring to, and what is its big-picture purpose?

5. The author listed various ways Jesus is the true tabernacle/temple, the great high priest, and the once-for-all sacrifice for sins. However, in a book of this size it is impossible to exhaust the New Testament teaching on these things. What are some other New Testament passages that speak to them? (For example, read Heb. 6:13–20 and explain especially v. 19.)

8

Unbelief

Delay for the Redeemed

WEEDING A GARDEN IS HARD WORK. To the novice it may *appear* easy: crawl through the garden, snap off the intruding weeds, and voilà, the front yard looks impressive. However, any experienced gardener knows that it isn't that simple: unless we pull up the root—every little piece of the root for every single weed—the weeds will return as quickly as they disappeared. And to get at the root we need to do the hard work of loosening the soil around a weed with a garden tool and then pulling the weed out ever so carefully. Otherwise part of the root will be left in the ground, and the plants we want to thrive will be choked out again. Effective weeding of a garden means completely uprooting each weed.

In many ways, a Christian's battle with sin resembles the hard work of weeding a garden. At first, it may seem easy: crawl through our spiritual lives, snapping off the intruding sins, and voilà, our external lives look impressive. However, any seasoned Christian knows that it isn't that simple: unless we kill sin at its root, it will return as quickly as it disappeared. In order to truly put sin to death, we need to do the hard work of getting down deep and identifying the "root" sins that manifest themselves in any number of other sins. This chapter is about one of the root sins that threatens to keep Christians from moving on to maturity, and even to pull them away from Christ.

In this chapter we are going to see that Israel's life in covenant with YHWH was not on a consistent "onward and upward" trajectory. Of the many examples we could draw from, we will notice that when it was time to move forward to receive the long-awaited fulfillment of YHWH's promises, the root sin of unbelief resulted in a forty-year delay.

This effort to notice the details of Israel's unbelief in the book of Numbers is a practical one. As the author of Hebrews put it, "Take care, brothers [and sisters], lest there be in any of you an evil, unbelieving heart, leading you to fall away from the living God" (Heb. 3:12). As we read about Israel's failures in the book of Numbers, we are invited to assess our own lives and "root out" any similar sins.

We will begin our chapter by getting a big-picture understanding of the book of Numbers before we look at the details of Israel's unbelief in more detail. We will also notice that YHWH's response to this unbelief was tempered with severe consequences as well as undeserved favor—grace. As we close, we will look a bit more at this theme from a New Testament perspective and ask what Jesus and the early Christians have to teach us about uprooting this sin in a way that results in God-glorifying, joy-filled, Christian maturity.

Numbers: The Big Picture

National Census

At the beginning and near the end of Numbers, Israel took a census. At this point many readers give up: the book is called "Numbers," and it records two separate cases of national census. Boring! As with most seemingly boring elements in the Bible, however, when we understand the reason for their inclusion, we can benefit from reading.

Numbers begins in the wilderness of Sinai. It had been a year and two months since the exodus from Egypt, and once again, YHWH spoke to Moses:

> Take a census of all the congregation of the people of Israel, by clans, by fathers' houses, according to the number of names, every male, head by head. From twenty years old and upward, all in Israel who are able to go to war, you and Aaron shall list them, company by company. (1:2–3)

Did you notice the clue? This was not a national census of the nation's *general* population. YHWH was not interested in the average number of kids per house or what zones of the Israelite camp may have needed more elementary schools. This was a census of *warriors*. Moses and Aaron were to make a list of everyone in Israel who was twenty years or older and able to go to war.

As we step back and remember the big-picture story of the Pentateuch, we understand why a census of warriors was needed: in judgment for the sins of the inhabitants of Canaan and in fulfillment of YHWH's covenant with Abraham (e.g., Gen. 15:12–16), YHWH was announcing that Israel would finally possess the promised land. And they would accomplish this by means of war. A census of warriors was needed—with a tribe-by-tribe list—so that the people could be organized for battle. So what about the second census found in Numbers 26? Between Numbers 1 and 26, nearly forty years elapsed, and the sin of unbelief prevailed. So the second census was of the next generation of warriors who would enter the promised land by faith and trust YHWH for the outcome. Whereas the first generation was marked by unbelief, the second generation would move forward in faith (as recorded in the book of Joshua).

Travel Diary

The next big-picture feature of Numbers is its travel diary. And once again, what may appear to be boring and irrelevant pops off the page when we understand its purpose. At the beginning of the book, Israel was in the wilderness of Sinai—their temporary home from Exodus 19:1 to Numbers 10:12. Then, beginning in Numbers 10:12, they traveled to Kadesh in the wilderness of Paran. Finally, in Numbers 22:1, they set out for the plains of Moab, where they stayed for the rest of the book. So what is the purpose of the travel diary? Israel was moving closer to the promised land. If we were to view this on a map, we would see God's people pressing northeast with each move so that by the end of Numbers, they were on the doorstep of Canaan. And it was at this point that Moses, in the book of Deuteronomy, would prepare the people to enter and possess the promised land.

Community Layout

There is still another "boring" feature of Numbers that communicates something important when we understand its purpose: the organization of Israel. The book of Numbers provides very detailed instructions on where each tribe of Israel was to camp or march when the people were settled or traveling. On one hand, this formation gave prominence to the tribe of Judah. Remember Genesis 49:10 and the promise that Judah's descendant would be a king over the community? As the generations unfolded—four hundred years after that promise was first made—the entire tribe of Judah had pride of place in the camp.

On the other hand, this formation made clear that the tabernacle was always central. When Israel was camping, they were organized *around* the tabernacle, with three tribes each on the north, east, south, and west. And when Israel was traveling, six tribes were to lead and six were to follow, and in between were the priests carrying the disassembled tabernacle. This meant that whether they were at camp or on the march, YHWH was central in Israel. While the special presence of YHWH had been lost after the fall into sin, these camping and marching formations represented a step toward restoration: Israel had YHWH dwelling in their midst (in the tabernacle) once again.

The Words of YHWH

Finally, there is a repeated phrase in Numbers that our eyes could easily skip over. Michael J. Glodo explains, "On no less than forty-one occasions, Numbers reports the contents of divine speech to Moses with the phrase 'the Lord spoke to Moses.'"[1] The point is simple: Israel was not left to grope for direction on their own. YHWH was *guiding* them toward the promised land. The faithful God of covenant promises was showing the way.

---

1 Michael J. Glodo, "Numbers," in *A Biblical-Theological Introduction to the Old Testament: The Gospel Promised*, ed. Miles V. Van Pelt (Wheaton, IL: Crossway, 2016), 110. Although Glodo did not capitalize all the letters in "Lord," in Hebrew this phrase reads "YHWH spoke to Moses," and so should more properly be translated as "the LORD spoke to Moses."

Unbelief and the Delayed Occupation of Canaan

Although the book of Numbers commenced with many encouragements, problems appeared in chapter 11, when the people began to complain about hardship. They bore YHWH's wrath for this sin, which was only abated by the intercession of Moses (Num. 11:1–2). The story of Numbers continued with complaints about food, along with a rebellion by Miriam and Aaron against Moses and his leadership (Num. 12). The scouting of Canaan came next, and this *should* have been a high point in the entire Pentateuch— Moses sent a leader from each tribe into Canaan and they came back overjoyed, but also overwhelmed (Num. 13). Specifically, they said:

> We came to the land to which you sent us. It flows with milk and honey, and this is its fruit. However, the people who dwell in the land are strong, and the cities are fortified and very large. And besides, we saw the descendants of Anak there. The Amalekites dwell in the land of the Negeb. The Hittites, the Jebusites, and the Amorites dwell in the hill country. And the Canaanites dwell by the sea, and along the Jordan. (13:27–29)

In short, they loved the land's abundance but were terrified of its inhabitants.

Although one man named Caleb responded in faith—"Let us go up at once and occupy it, for we are well able to overcome it" (13:30)—he was the lone voice in the midst of unbelief. In response to Caleb:

> The men who had gone up with him said, "We are not able to go up against the people, for they are stronger than we are." So they brought to the people of Israel a bad report of the land that

they had spied out, saying, "The land, through which we have gone to spy it out, is a land that devours its inhabitants, and all the people that we saw in it are of great height. And there we saw the Nephilim (the sons of Anak, who come from the Nephilim), and we seemed to ourselves like grasshoppers, and so we seemed to them. (Num. 13:31–33)

With the unbelief of the leaders, the people followed, even claiming it would be better to return to Egypt (14:3). In response, Joshua and Caleb sought to counter-lead with words of faith:

The land, which we passed through to spy it out, is an exceedingly good land. If the LORD delights in us, he will bring us into this land and give it to us, a land that flows with milk and honey. Only do not rebel against the LORD. And do not fear the people of the land, for they are bread for us. Their protection is removed from them, and the LORD is with us; do not fear them. (14:7–9)

When we remember that this land had been *promised* by YHWH, we can understand why not entering in faith was tantamount to rebellion—with their actions, the people showed that they did not believe YHWH was a covenant-keeping God. In fact, the very people who had just experienced the exodus from Egypt and the overthrow of the mightiest army in the ancient world were now doubting whether YHWH could overpower the strong inhabitants of Canaan. As Morales put it, "Because Israel did not fear YHWH they would fear their enemies."[2] And before we look down our

2   L. Michael Morales, *Who Shall Ascend the Mountain of the Lord? A Biblical Theology of the Book of Leviticus*, New Studies in Biblical Theology 37, ed. D. A. Carson (Downers Grove, IL: InterVarsity Press, 2015), 222.

noses at these people, how many of us have experienced great blessing and deliverance from God and then responded with unbelief at much lesser obstacles than a group of fortified cities and their strong inhabitants?

This sets up the scene for the response of YHWH. The whole community threatened to murder Joshua and Moses. Then YHWH's glory appeared to all the Israelites at the tent of meeting (14:10). In the scene that follows, YHWH first assessed the situation in the form of a series of questions: "How long will this people despise me? And how long will they not believe in me, in spite of all the signs that I have done among them?" (14:11). Notice that to *not believe* in YHWH in spite of all the signs he had done among the people was tantamount to *despising* him. In light of this assessment, YHWH spoke words of judgment that the community deserved: "I will strike them with the pestilence and disinherit them, and I will make of you [Moses] a nation greater and mightier than they" (Num. 14:12).

However, Moses interceded once again, appealing to the fact that the Egyptians would hear of this and misinterpret the outcome: although Israel would be judged for their unbelief, the nations would *think* that they were killed in the wilderness because of YHWH's inability to save (14:13–16). Instead, Moses appealed to YHWH's character as it was first revealed in Exodus 34:6–7:

And now, please let the power of the Lord be great as you have promised, saying, "The LORD is slow to anger and abounding in steadfast love, forgiving iniquity and transgression, but he will by no means clear the guilty, visiting the iniquity of the fathers on the children, to the third and the fourth generation." Please pardon the iniquity of this people, according to the greatness of your steadfast love, just as you have forgiven this people, from Egypt until now. (14:17–19)

This scene does not teach us to bring our entitled attitude to YHWH; it teaches us to desperately appeal to YHWH's revealed character as we seek forgiveness for our sins.

Although YHWH did pardon the sin of the community, he also brought consequences for their sin of unbelief. He said:

> I have pardoned, according to your word. But truly, as I live, and as all the earth shall be filled with the glory of the LORD, none of the men who have seen my glory and my signs that I did in Egypt and in the wilderness, and yet have put me to the test these ten times and have not obeyed my voice, shall see the land that I swore to give to their fathers. And none of those who despised me shall see it. But my servant Caleb, because he has a different spirit and has followed me fully, I will bring into the land into which he went, and his descendants shall possess it. (14:20–24)

In short, the unbelief of the exodus generation would result in forty years of funerals in the wilderness—with the exceptions of Caleb and Joshua, every fighting man twenty or older would die before the community could enter the promised land (14:26–30). As Andrew J. Schmutzer put it, "Due to their faithless rebellion against Yahweh and his prophet Moses, a venture that should have taken weeks instead took forty years. How quickly redeemed people can forget the greatness and holiness of their God!"[3] Although the

---

3 Andrew J. Schmutzer, "Numbers," in *What the Old Testament Authors Really Cared About: A Survey of Jesus' Bible*, ed. Jason S. DeRouchie (Grand Rapids, MI: Kregel Academic, 2013), 138.

ten spies died instantly, the rest of the people would live out their days until the next generation could enter the promised land forty years later (14:37–38).

Although we may think the scene should have ended there, it does not. In response to these words of judgment, the people mourned, rose early, and gathered to enter the promised land after all (14:39–40). Although Moses warned them that YHWH would not be with them in this mission, they went anyway and were handily defeated before their foes (14:41–45). Without the blessing of YHWH, the entry into the land of promise would never succeed. From this we learn that unbelief can result in inaction (being frozen in fear, as in Num. 14:1–38), or action (presumptuously going out to fight, as in Num. 14:39–45). More failures would follow in the book of Numbers—including the unbelief of Moses and Aaron in Numbers 20:12. It was clear that blessing would come only after the forty years of funerals were complete. In fact, not even Moses or Aaron would enter the land, though Moses would prepare the community for such an entry and see the land from a distance before he died outside the land of promise.

A Scepter and a Star: Hope in the Darkness

In light of the story so far, we might have expected the book of Numbers to be completely bleak from start to finish, but this is gloriously not the case. YHWH is indeed a holy God who will by no means clear the guilty (Ex. 34:7), but he is also merciful and gracious, slow to anger, and abounding in steadfast love and faithfulness (34:6). In short, the God of the covenant loves to lavish blessing on his undeserving people.

Along the way in the book of Numbers, YHWH not only allowed the unbelief of the people to result in delay instead of destitution; he also provided for relief from a plague (Num. 21:4–9; cf. John 3:14–16). Also, when the king of Moab hired the prophet Balaam to put a curse on Israel, YHWH turned it into multiple blessings in four separate oracles (Num. 22–24). A second census then signaled the end of the forty years of funerals and the beginning of a new generation who would believe YHWH, taking him at his word (Num. 26). And from the beginning to the end of Numbers, YHWH also continued to provide the daily food for his people and guided them by a cloud in the daylight and a pillar of fire by night. He also continued the leadership of Moses, along with the provisions of a functioning tabernacle, priesthood, and sacrificial system. Against the black-velvet backdrop of the community's unbelief in Numbers, the diamond of YHWH's grace shone all the more brightly. He truly was (and is) the God of amazing grace!

Although space restrictions will not allow us to unpack all of these blessings, we will take a look at Balaam's fourth oracle to Israel. Before we cite it, we do well to remember that it came from a non-Israelite prophet who was not—and never would be—in covenant relationship with YHWH. As Schmutzer put it, "The Bible consistently portrays Balaam as a false teacher, greedy for profit (Josh. 13:22; 2 Peter 2:15; Jude 11)."[4] In other words, the lesson from the four Balaam oracles is that YHWH could even direct words of blessing on his people from a *pagan* prophet. In fact, he could even open the mouth of a donkey to provide direction (Num. 22:22–35).

It is this Balaam who spoke a fourth time:

The oracle of Balaam the son of Beor, the oracle of the man whose eye is opened, the oracle of him who hears the words of God, and knows the knowledge of the Most High, who sees the

4 Schmutzer, "Numbers," 127.

vision of the Almighty, falling down with his eyes uncovered: I see him, but not now; I behold him, but not near: a star shall come out of Jacob, and a scepter shall rise out of Israel; it shall crush the forehead of Moab and break down all the sons of Sheth. Edom shall be dispossessed; Seir also, his enemies, shall be dispossessed. Israel is doing valiantly. And one from Jacob shall exercise dominion and destroy the survivors of cities! (24:15–19)

This oracle reported the words of God, the Most High, the Almighty. And it spoke of one who would come in the distant future—he was "not near."

As we notice the details of this prophetic word, three different images from the book of Genesis shed light on its meaning. First, this one would be a star out of Jacob. This reminds us of YHWH's promise that Abraham's descendants would be as numerous as the stars of the sky (Gen. 15:5). Therefore, Balaam's coming one would be one from among those "stars"; he would be a descendant of Abraham.[5]

Second, this coming one would also be a scepter who rose out of Israel. This reminds us of Jacob's blessing on Judah in Genesis 49:10. Therefore, we can see that this "individual star" from the descendants of Abraham would also be a king who would rule over the people of God. Although this may at first appear to point to King David, the "not near" nature of his coming seems better directed to another coming one, beyond David's comparatively imminent reign.[6]

5 See Stephen G. Dempster, *Dominion and Dynasty: A Theology of the Hebrew Bible*, New Studies in Biblical Theology 15, ed. D. A. Carson (Downers Grove, IL: InterVarsity Press, 2003), 116–17.

6 See John H. Sailhamer, *The Pentateuch as Narrative: A Biblical-Theological Commentary*, Library of Biblical Interpretation (Grand Rapids, MI: Zondervan, 1992), 409.

As we notice what this star/scepter would accomplish, a third image from Genesis comes to mind. In the oracle, this coming one would provide defeat of Israel's enemies, those who kept God's people from the blessing of experiencing a full return to Eden. In the language of Genesis 3:15, we can say that this star/scepter would also be the ultimate offspring of the woman who would crush the head of the offspring of the serpent. He would win the ultimate victory over the serpent and the horrible impact his temptation had on human history after Eden.[7]

In summary, this was a prophecy about the coming Messiah, the coming Israelite ("star"), who would be King of the Jews ("scepter"), and who would win the ultimate victory over Satan, sin, death, and hell for God's people ("victorious warrior"). The hope expressed in the book of Numbers is not merely a temporal note of temporal mercy to a people who deserved immediate wrath; it also offers a long-range promise of ultimate salvation for those who will turn from their sin of unbelief and trust the God who is faithful to his covenant promises.

Looking Forward to Christ: "I Believe, Help My Unbelief!"

We have already been pointed to the coming Messiah in our reading of Numbers. As the author of Hebrews reflected on the scene of unbelief in Numbers, however, he also saw direct application to the Christian life:

> Take care, brothers [and sisters], lest there be in any of you an evil, unbelieving heart, leading you to fall away from the living God. But exhort one another every day, as long as it is called "today," that none of you may be hardened by the deceitfulness

---

7   See Dempster, *Dominion and Dynasty*, 117.

of sin. For we have come to share in Christ, if indeed we hold our original confidence firm to the end. As it is said, "Today, if you hear his voice, do not harden your hearts as in the rebellion." For who were those who heard and yet rebelled? Was it not all those who left Egypt led by Moses? And with whom was he provoked for forty years? Was it not with those who sinned, whose bodies fell in the wilderness? And to whom did he swear that they would not enter his rest, but to those who were disobedient? So we see that they were unable to enter because of unbelief. (Heb. 3:12–19)

To summarize, Christians should read the book of Numbers and stand in fear. We should see that none of us is beyond the "root sin" of unbelief that can manifest itself in so many other sins. Ultimately, this sin is capable of leading us to fall away from the living God. So the million-dollar question is, How can we fight against this sin? Hebrews clearly tells us: *Christians need each other!*

According to Hebrews 3, in contrast to the sin of unbelief, Christians need to exhort (or encourage) one another every day. This will result in none of us being hardened by the deceitfulness of sin. We also need to remember that only those who finish "in Christ" are currently sharers in his blessings—a sign of authentic salvation is endurance to the end. If the fearful from the book of Numbers were not able to enter the promised land because of their unbelief, how much more should we read and fear the same outcome in our journey toward the new heavens and the new earth where righteousness dwells. Christians need to gather regularly to spur one another on to endurance. This means of grace will result in the glorious outcome that is our ultimate hope.

As we close, there is one final dose of reality to consider: our hearts are easily prone to unbelief. Since none of us is beyond this "root sin," we should always remain vigilant in our fight against it. We have seen that one essential way of battling this sin is by regularly gathering with Christians—even daily hearing words that encourage us in Christ. Another incredible (and freeing) weapon in our fight against this sin is to pray the prayer of a man who struggled to believe that Jesus could heal his daughter: "Immediately the father of the child cried out and said, 'I believe; help my unbelief!'" (Mark 9:24). It is freeing to confess our struggle to the Lord, even as we continue to pursue the blessing of Christian community in the midst of this fight.

Discussion Questions

1. Using a gardening illustration, the author suggested that unbelief is a "root sin." What did he mean? Can you think of some ways that this sin might sprout up and manifest itself in a number of other sins?

2. The author shared some details about the big picture of Numbers that may seem boring and irrelevant at first but are shown to be important and even edifying once we understand their purpose. Did any of these stick out to you as particularly helpful? Share with your group.

3. Although it is easy for twenty-first-century readers to "look down our noses" at Israel's unbelief, the author suggested that it is just as easy for us to slip into this sin. If you are comfortable, share with the group a specific way you might be tempted down this dangerous road of unbelief.

4. In the midst of the black-velvet bleakness of Israel's sin, the author suggested that the diamond of YHWH's grace in Numbers shines all the more brightly. Were you particularly surprised by any of these displays of grace? Share with the group.

5. Which three passages from Genesis shed light on Balaam's fourth oracle? Explain.

6. According to the letter to the Hebrews, Christians need to beware of falling into the sin of unbelief. What are some practices Hebrews 3 points out that can guard against us falling into this horrible "root sin"?

9

Blessings and Curses

Warning the Redeemed

WHEN MANY CHRISTIANS ARE ASKED to list the most important books of the Old Testament, their minds tend to gravitate toward Isaiah and its predictions about the coming Messiah, the Psalms as songs/prayers that led to the coming Savior, and Genesis as the book of beginnings. The books of 1 and 2 Samuel may also come to mind, since they tell the story of King David and YHWH's covenant with him. The book of Exodus may come to mind because it tells the story of Israel's exodus from Egypt, the Ten Commandments, and the beginnings of tabernacle worship. Proverbs may also make the list, with its practical instructions about wise living in covenant with YHWH. But it is unlikely that many Christians would think about the book of Deuteronomy as one of the most important.

Actually, if we were to travel back in time to the years leading up to the birth of Jesus, we would find that any Jewish leader would have thought immediately of Deuteronomy as very prominent. Other books would also have come to mind—especially Isaiah, Genesis, and Psalms—but Deuteronomy would likely have risen to the highest place of prominence. In fact, Deuteronomy could be likened to Romans—while Romans is the magnum opus of the apostle Paul, Deuteronomy is the same for Moses. Years after it was originally written, when Josiah rediscovered the book of the *torah* of YHWH, the book of Deuteronomy was what he found (see 2 Kings 22). Years later still, when Jesus was in the wilderness undergoing temptations by Satan, he rebuffed each of the three temptations by quoting the book of Deuteronomy (see Matt. 4:1–11). Christians often think about Deuteronomy as a mere recap of Genesis, Exodus, Leviticus, and Numbers, with a bit of extra material along the way. But the book is so much more than a mere recapping of material. Although this book does begin with a look back, it also provides essential instruction for living as YHWH's redeemed people in the promised land.

In this chapter we will gain a big-picture sense of Deuteronomy before we zero in on one element of its teaching that has particular bearing on our study. As usual, we'll close by looking forward to Christ in light of what we have learned.

Deuteronomy: The Big Picture

Three Speeches

The bulk of Deuteronomy consists of three long speeches by Moses. The book starts this way: "These are the words that Moses spoke to all Israel beyond the Jordan in the wilderness" (Deut. 1:1). In this section, Moses led Israel in a backward gaze so that they could remember the place from which YHWH had brought them.

Next, Deuteronomy 4:44 contains a second marker of a long speech: "This is the law that Moses set before the people of Israel." This long section makes up the bulk of the book of Deuteronomy, and it instructed Israel how to live as the redeemed people of YHWH in the promised land. Since Moses would die outside of the promised land, these words were needed as the constitution of the nation in its new land.

Finally, in Deuteronomy 29:1 we find the beginning of Moses's third long speech: "These are the words of the covenant that the LORD commanded Moses to make [literally, *cut*] with the people of Israel in the land of Moab, besides the covenant that he had made [literally, *cut*] with them at Horeb." Although at first glance this sounds like YHWH was initiating (or "cutting") a fresh covenant with Moses/Israel, Peter Gentry suggests that in this passage, YHWH was prompting Israel to make a covenant to keep the previous covenant.[1] In other words, Deuteronomy was a "supplement to the covenant at Sinai" that was narrated in the book of Exodus.[2] This book was a call to abide by the terms of YHWH's covenant with Moses/Israel as they entered their new life situation, when the promises of a nation with its own land would be fulfilled.

An Exposition of the Torah

Another way of understanding Deuteronomy is through the lens of one of its first verses: "Beyond the Jordan, in the land of Moab, Moses undertook to explain this law, saying . . ." (1:5). The first thing we notice is the location of this speech by Moses: "beyond the Jordan [River], in the land of Moab." Although most of us do not have a mental map of the ancient Near East, we can observe that the most important thing about this statement was where it did *not* take place: in the land of Canaan. The fact that it took place

---

1 See Peter J. Gentry and Stephen J. Wellum, *Kingdom through Covenant: A Biblical-Theological Understanding of the Covenants*, 2nd ed. (Wheaton, IL: Crossway, 2018), 419.

2 Gentry and Wellum, *Kingdom through Covenant*, 418.

"beyond the Jordan" also emphasized that it was close to Canaan, but not in it. By the time Deuteronomy began, the forty years of wilderness wanderings had concluded, and Israel was poised to enter the promised land of Canaan; they were at its very border.

In this location we also learn what Moses did: he "undertook to explain this law." By this point in our study of the Pentateuch, we know that the law, or *torah*, refers to YHWH's instruction on how to live as his redeemed people. We have witnessed this instruction in the latter half of Exodus, and in the books of Leviticus and Numbers. And now as YHWH's people were poised to enter and occupy the promised land, Moses undertook to explain this instruction, this *torah*. The Hebrew verb translated "to explain" means something along the lines of "to make clear" or "to make plain" or "to explain." On the border of Canaan, Moses explained the *torah* of YHWH; like a good preacher he made sure the people understood it. In order to prepare them to enter the promised land, they needed to grasp the instruction of YHWH so they could live it out.

A Treaty Document

As scholars have studied the ancient scrolls of Israel's neighbors, they have noticed similarities between the structure of Deuteronomy and some of these documents. In an earlier chapter we noticed that covenants between people were common in Old Testament times. Just as there is a common structure and content in many contracts in our day, so in the ancient Near East there was a common order and content for these covenants. Specifically, many scholars have noticed similarities between Deuteronomy and covenants between a stronger party and a weaker party in the documents of Israel's neighbors, a covenant technically called a "suzerain-vassal treaty."

Even more specifically, the structure and content of Deuteronomy resembles most the suzerain-vassal treaties of the Hittite people, Israel's neighbors at the same time Moses was alive. Carmen Imes helpfully summarizes the similarities:

> While Deuteronomy is not itself a treaty document, it bears some similarity with other ancient Near Eastern treaties. Like Hittite treaties, Deuteronomy's recital of the covenant includes a title (1:1–5); a historical prologue (1:6–4:49); a list of stipulations (chapters 5–26); instructions for depositing the document in the temple (31:9–13); description of the ceremony (chapter 27); a list of witnesses (31:26); and blessings and curses (chapter 28).[3]

It makes sense that Moses would adopt this structure when he was creating a constitution for Israel. The people would be familiar with the general structure of the document and would also be able to make sense of its unique content. In the book of Deuteronomy, the great suzerain (YHWH) was restating the terms of his covenant with his vassal (Israel).

Blessings, Curses, and Restoration: An Introduction

Although a thorough study of every detail in Deuteronomy is beyond the scope of this book, and although comparing Deuteronomy with other ancient Near Eastern covenants can be a fruitful study, in this final chapter of our book we are going to focus on three unique points from the end of Deuteronomy that act as our "reading glasses" for understanding the rest of the

3 Carmen Joy Imes, *Bearing God's Name: Why Sinai Still Matters* (Downers Grove, IL: IVP Academic, 2019), 61.

Old Testament. Just as those of us who wear corrective lenses see the world more clearly when those lenses are in front of our eyes, so readers of the Old Testament will understand Joshua, Judges, 1 and 2 Samuel, 1 and 2 Kings, the Prophetic Books, 1 and 2 Chronicles, and many other Old Testament books better when they read them through the lenses of Deuteronomy 28 and Deuteronomy 30:1–10.

Near the conclusion of the book, Deuteronomy 28:1–14 motivated Israel with a wonderful list of blessings for covenant-keeping. Then Deuteronomy 28:15–68 warned Israel with a horrifying list of curses for covenant-breaking. Finally, Deuteronomy 30:1–10 instructed Israel with a gracious word about restoration for covenant repentance.[4]

As we look ahead in the word of God, these three portions of Deuteronomy explain the coming possession of the promised land with the temple as a permanent, central place of worship for God's people (blessings). They also explain the subsequent division of God's people into Judah and Israel, the wars they would face, and the defeat and expulsion from the promised land that each of these two nations would suffer (curses). For example, 1 Chronicles 9:1 makes clear the link between unfaithfulness to the covenant and the Babylonian exile: "Judah was taken into exile in Babylon *because of their breach of faith.*" Finally, Deuteronomy 30:1–10 explains why the people of Israel could, while under the curse of YHWH in exile, still approach YHWH to ask for deliverance (restoration). It also explains how they were enabled to return to the promised land,

---

4 It is also worth pointing out that Lev. 26 contains these same three points: blessings for covenant-keeping (Lev. 26:3–13), curses for covenant-breaking (Lev. 26:14–39), and restoration for covenant repentance (Lev. 26:40–45). Therefore, Moses's words at the end of Deuteronomy reiterate this teaching for the new generation of Israelites.

build a second temple, and live once again in the place YHWH had promised to Abraham.

The Covenant as the Foundation

Before we look more closely at the blessings for covenant-keeping, curses for covenant-breaking, and restoration for covenant repentance, we need to recall that all these teachings were rooted in the covenant between YHWH and Moses/Israel. And we recall from the chapter on *torah* that Exodus 19–24 was not meant to teach Israel how to *become* YHWH's special people. Instead, it instructed Israel about how to live as YHWH's people in light of the fact that YHWH had redeemed them from Egypt and brought them to himself (Ex. 19:4). Since the covenant was rooted in grace, and since it instructed those who were already YHWH's people, it was not about *getting in*, but *living as*. Deuteronomy 28:1–68 and 30:1–10 built on this and basically taught, "You are already YHWH's people; it will go very well with you if you keep the terms of the covenant that he set with you. It will go very poorly with you if you break the terms of this same covenant; but there is hope in the midst of covenant curses because he will restore the disobedient if they repent from their covenant-breaking." With these things in mind, we are ready to take a closer look.

Blessings for Covenant-Keeping

Deuteronomy 28:1–14 begins this way: "If you faithfully obey the voice of the LORD your God, being careful to do all his commandments that I command you today, the LORD your God will set you high above all the nations of the earth. And all these blessings shall come upon you and overtake you, if you obey the voice of the LORD your God."

I can remember touchdowns I scored during tackle football games (with no protective equipment!) when I was in grade school. I was small and fast, so I knew that if I just kept running I could make it through the game. But I also knew that if anyone overtook me, I might have needed the care of doctors. Thankfully, although there were many stronger boys in my class, none could run faster than I, so I was rarely overtaken in these situations. The image in Deuteronomy 28, however, is of an entire people being pursued and overtaken *by blessings*. As they faithfully obeyed (or kept) the voice of YHWH their God (i.e., the terms of the covenant YHWH articulated through Moses), blessings would pursue them and overtake them and be theirs.

As the passage continues, we see that whoever they were, whatever they owned, whatever they did, and wherever they went would be blessed. These blessings would come in city and field to their children, their ground, and their livestock's offspring (28:3–4). Their basket and kneading bowl, their coming in and going out, would all be blessed (28:5–6). YHWH would cause them to have victory over their enemies (28:7). Their barns and all that they undertook would be blessed, and he would bless them in the land he was about to give them (28:8).

Next, YHWH promised more blessing and also reminded Israel of their part in this glorious outcome: "The LORD will establish you as a people holy [or consecrated] to himself, as he has sworn to you, if you keep the commandments of the LORD your God and walk in his ways. And all the peoples of the earth shall see that you are called by the name of the LORD, and they shall be afraid of you" (Deut. 28:9–10).

And then the promises of blessing continued: YHWH would cause them to abound in prosperity in terms of children and livestock and crops, all within the land YHWH swore to give their fathers (28:11). YHWH would give them rain and bless all the work of their hands. They would also lend to nations but never borrow; Israel would be the head and not the tail, and they would go up and not down. Once again, this was all dependent on them keeping the covenant: ". . . if you obey the commandments of the LORD your God, which I command you today, being careful to do them, and if you do not turn aside from any of the words that I command you today, to the right hand or to the left, to go after other gods to serve them" (Deut. 28:13–14). At the conclusion of this passage, we notice that keeping the covenant also involved never going after any of the gods of the nations. With such lavish blessings for covenant-keeping, Israel had a lot of motivation to remain faithful to YHWH.

Curses for Covenant-Breaking

Deuteronomy 28 continues with curses for covenant-breaking in verses 15–68—the bulk of the chapter. As we dive in, let's remember that the graphic descriptions of the curses were not portraits of random tragedies. In Deuteronomy 28:15–68 there was a clear link between the graphic tragedy and the hand of YHWH—the one who would send the curse of the covenant on all who broke it. Disregarding the instruction of YHWH would result in tragic consequences. But this section of Scripture was far from being a doomsday prediction. Instead, it functioned to *warn* the redeemed, to show them graphically what would happen to those who did not live out the instruction of YHWH as he prescribed. As Jason S. DeRouchie put it, "The curses were ultimately blessings in disguise for all who would learn from them—the gracious disciplining hand of a loving covenant 'king' (Deut 33:5) or 'father' (1:31; 32:6) designed to shake Israel out of their ignorance and to draw them back to the Lord (8:5; cf. Heb 12:5–11)."[5]

The transitional verse, 28:15, reads, "But if you will not obey the voice of the LORD your God or be careful to do all his commandments and his statutes that I command you today, then all these curses shall come upon you and overtake you." Just as blessings would overtake those who kept the covenant, in this passage curses would overtake those who broke the covenant. Covenant breakers would be cursed wherever they were, in whatever they owned, and whatever they did—in the city or field; basket and kneading bowl; children, crops, and livestock; coming and going (28:16–19).

Life in rebellion against the covenant would be frustrating and painful and would end in death: "The LORD will send on you curses, confusion, and frustration in all that you undertake to do, until you are destroyed and perish quickly on account of the evil of your deeds, because you have forsaken me" (28:20). They would be victims of disease, drought, and mildew (28:21–24). They would be defeated in battle, and instead of a proper burial their dead bodies would be eaten by scavenging animals. Those who lived would suffer at the hands of boils and tumors and scabs and itch with no relief. Their minds would be confused and out of touch with reality. They would have no relief from oppression (28:25–29). In the midst of this were the chilling words, ". . . and there shall be no one to help you" (28:29). YHWH would not be there when they called out in desperation.

The passage continues with a series of reversals in which everything they worked toward would be taken from them. They would

---

5 Jason S. DeRouchie, "Deuteronomy," in *What the Old Testament Authors Really Cared About: A Survey of Jesus' Bible*, ed. Jason S. DeRouchie (Grand Rapids, MI: Kregel Academic, 2013), 155.

be engaged to a wife but another would sleep with her; they would build a house but would not live in it; they would plant a vineyard, but someone else would harvest it; their ox would be slaughtered, but they would not eat it; their donkey and sheep would be taken from them; their sons and daughters would be given to another people (28:30–32). As another nation ate their crops, they would be driven to madness, but in the face of this YHWH would strike them with incurable boils across their entire body (28:33–35). Life would be miserable, and the curses would be from YHWH.

Next, there was no relief for the pain; it would only get worse. Beginning in 28:36 Israel learned that another curse for covenant-breaking would be exile from the promised land. Although the loss of one's house and a forced move to another country would be tragic for anyone, this curse needs to be read in light of the entire purpose of the promised land: Israel had YHWH dwelling in their midst. If the promised land was a first step toward a return to Eden, the result of covenant-breaking would be a move farther away from the Bible's end goal. Another nation would bring them and their king to their land, and there YHWH's people would serve other gods of wood and stone (28:36). In that place they would become a pathetic people at whom others would stare in horror. They would plant lots of seed that locusts would eat, plant vineyards that worms would eat, plant olive trees with olives that would drop off, and father children who would go into captivity. Also, the cricket would possess their trees and crops, and the sojourner among them would rise higher than they, lending *them* money (28:37–44).

A summary statement comes next:

All these curses shall come upon you and pursue you and over-take you till you are destroyed, because you did not obey the voice of the LORD your God, to keep his commandments and his statutes that he commanded you. They shall be a sign and a wonder against you and your offspring forever. Because you did not serve the LORD your God with joyfulness and gladness of heart, because of the abundance of all things, therefore you shall serve your enemies whom the LORD will send against you, in hunger and thirst, in nakedness, and lacking everything. And he will put a yoke of iron on your neck until he has destroyed you. (28:45–48)

The passage continues with more vivid images of exile, as their victor would not show respect to their old or mercy to their young. The victors would eat their livestock and crops; they would break down the city walls in which Israel trusted and besiege them in all their towns throughout the land that YHWH their God had given them (28:49–52).

Next, the vivid images of suffering in exile get worse: they would be so starved that they would eat their own children. They would hide the flesh of their children they were eating from their brother, wife, and other children, and the most delicate women among them would hide the afterbirth from her family so she could eat it herself (28:53–57). What is more, the diseases they feared in Egypt would cling to them until they were destroyed. In a stark reversal of the blessing to Abraham, "whereas you were as numerous as the stars of heaven, you shall be left few in number, because you did not obey the voice of the LORD your God" (28:62).

As YHWH took delight in doing good to them when they were keeping the covenant, he would take delight in bringing ruin upon them if they broke it (28:63). Outside the land, YHWH would scatter them among all peoples, from one end of the earth to the other, and there they would serve other gods of wood and stone (28:64). In these places they would find no respite, and YHWH would give them "a trembling heart and failing eyes and a languishing soul" (28:65). They would have no security that they would live through each day, and they would live in dread with no relief. And to cap it off, they learned that "the LORD will bring you back in ships to Egypt, a journey that I promised that you should never make again; and there you shall offer yourselves for sale to your enemies as male and female slaves, but there will be no buyer" (28:68).

This has been a horrible, painful mouthful, and these words were meant as a *blessing* to YHWH's people: they were to soak in these horrors as a means of being spurred on to remaining faithful to YHWH. Their God was indeed merciful, "gracious, slow to anger, and abounding in steadfast love and faithfulness, who kept steadfast love for thousands." But he was also a God "who will by no means clear the guilty, visiting the iniquity of the fathers on the children and the children's children, to the third and the fourth generation" (Ex. 34:6–7).

Restoration for Covenant Repentance

After a covenant summary in Deuteronomy 29 come awesome words of promise in the next chapter. In Deuteronomy 30:1–10 Israel learned the precious truth that if they found themselves in a situation where they were groaning under the curses for covenant-breaking, they were not hopeless, for YHWH also promised them restoration for covenant repentance. This meant that the same God who took delight in bringing these curses upon them (28:63)—because he would be glorified as a God of *justice*—was also one to whom they could cry out in the midst of this same suffering. What God is there like this? As he was bringing justice

to bear for covenant-breaking, he would be a refuge who promised restoration if they would repent. He truly is "a God merciful
and gracious, slow to anger, and abounding in steadfast love and
faithfulness" (Ex. 34:6).

Deuteronomy 30 begins with a scene of exile, as Israel was under
the curse for covenant-breaking (v. 1). In that exile, YHWH said
that if they would

> return to the LORD your God, you and your children, and obey
> his voice in all that I command you today, with all your heart
> and with all your soul, then [YHWH] your God will restore
> your fortunes and have mercy on you, and he will gather you
> again from all the peoples where the LORD your God has scat-
> tered you. (30:2–3)

Restoration could be theirs if they would repent. In fact, YHWH
would gather the farthest flung of his people and bring them back
to possess their land, and he would make them more numerous
than their fathers (30:4–5). It sounds like a full restoration of the
blessings promised to Abraham. What is more, YHWH would
circumcise their hearts and the hearts of their children "so that you
will love the LORD your God with all your heart and with all your
soul, that you may live" (30:6).

In a stunning case of reversal, YHWH would put all of these
curses on their enemies who persecuted them, and Israel would
again obey the voice of YHWH and keep all his commandments
(30:7–8). He would restore their prosperity in all areas—work,
children, livestock, harvest—and he would again take delight in
prospering them when they obeyed the voice of YHWH their
God, when they once again kept his covenant and had turned to

him with all their heart and with all their soul (30:9–10). Praise YHWH for this hope!

The Rest of the Story: How the Warnings Played Out in Israel's History

As was suggested at the beginning of this chapter, when we read beyond the book of Deuteronomy, we find these three themes—blessings for covenant-keeping, curses for covenant-breaking, and restoration for covenant repentance—played out in the rest of the Old Testament. In the book of Joshua, Israel did possess the promised land, and in the book of Samuel they were centralized with a king in Jerusalem. In 1 Kings a temple was built—a place of greater permanence where YHWH could dwell in the midst of his people. Through the lens of Deuteronomy 28:1–14, the blessings for covenant-keeping were certainly lavished on God's people.

However, covenant-breaking was also a nagging reality through the period of the Judges, in the early chapters of 1 Samuel, and in the latter portion of David's life. Although Solomon started out well, his heart was enticed by his many foreign wives to serve other gods (cf. Deut. 17:17). And after his death the kingdom was split in two, and things went from bad to worse. Although the southern kingdom of Judah did have various godly kings, the majority were evil. And the northern kingdom of Israel had all evil kings who led the people's hearts away from YHWH. So the curses for covenant-breaking were brought upon the disobedient people of YHWH. First, in 722 BC, the northern kingdom of Israel fell to the Assyrians and God's people were exiled from their land. Next, in 586/587 BC, the southern kingdom of Judah fell to the Babylonians and they were exiled from their land. In a horrifying scene, the glory of YHWH left the temple before the wicked king Nebuchadnezzar and his army destroyed it and stripped the gold, jewels, and other valuables from it to be carried back to Babylon (2 Kings 25).

The people of YHWH were left without a land, without a king, without a temple, and without hope. Almost. If they'd been left without Deuteronomy 30:1–10, they would have been completely without hope, but armed with this passage, and led by faithful examples such as Esther, Daniel, Ezra, and Nehemiah, they learned faithfulness to YHWH in the midst of exile. And then they were led back to the promised land to reestablish their territory, their temple, and their covenant commitment to YHWH. Although the Old Testament ended on a note of yearning, because the full return from exile had not yet been accomplished, the measure of restoration God's people had experienced was tangible and hope-giving. Their God was faithfully restoring them on the basis of their covenant repentance.

Looking Forward to Christ: Warnings for Christians in the Book of Hebrews

Throughout this book we have reflected on the various ways Jesus fulfilled the hope of the Old Testament. In light of our study in this chapter, we can put it another way: in Jesus, YHWH's people experienced the full restoration for covenant repentance. Although the Old Testament return from exile did not include the restoration of a king on David's throne, Jesus came as the King who died in our place (note the sign hung on his cross) and after rising from the dead, ascended to heaven, and is now seated at the right hand of God's throne (cf. Ps. 110:4; Heb. 10:12). Although the second temple established in Ezra–Nehemiah was smaller and less glorious than the one built by Solomon, the hope of a better temple (cf. Ezek. 40–48) was fulfilled first in Jesus, who tabernacled among us and whose body was the temple (John 1:14; 2:21). This hope was fulfilled next in Christ's people, who are temples of the Holy Spirit (1 Cor. 3:16; 6:19). And a day is coming when the new Jerusalem will have no temple because it will be an enormous Most Holy Place, a true return to a new and better garden of Eden, where YHWH will dwell with his people forever. We could go on. There is hope because of Jesus.

As we think about the Christian life, however, we find that new-covenant believers in Jesus are also blessed with warnings. If Deuteronomy 28:15–68 taught us that it can and should be a blessing to reflect on vivid, horrifying displays of what will come to those who abandon the covenant, the book of Hebrews teaches us something similar about the Christian life. Although we could say much about this, we have space for just one example. After calling his Christian readers to maturity in Christ, the author warned:

> It is impossible, in the case of those who have once been enlightened, who have tasted the heavenly gift, and have shared in the Holy Spirit, and have tasted the goodness of the word of God and the powers of the age to come, and then have fallen away, to restore them again to repentance, since they are crucifying once again the Son of God to their own harm and holding him up to contempt. For land that has drunk the rain that often falls on it, and produces a crop useful to those for whose sake it is cultivated, receives a blessing from God. But if it bears thorns and thistles, it is worthless and near to being cursed, and its end is to be burned. (Heb. 6:4–8)

Christians should live with a healthy dose of fear, even as the author goes on to say that he and his fellow leaders were confident that these things would not come upon those who read this letter. So why did he add this stark warning? Because the warning would be part of the means God used to keep them faithful to Christ to the end. Scriptural warnings are given as blessings for the redeemed to spur them on to endurance in Christ to the end.

Discussion Questions

1. Prior to reading this chapter, if you had been asked to list the most important books of the Old Testament, what would you have said? Where would Deuteronomy have factored on your list (if at all)?

2. The author observed that Deuteronomy largely consists in three long speeches by Moses. Have you ever heard it broken up this way? Does this broad breakdown help you to navigate the contents of the book?

3. The author observed that the book of Deuteronomy bears many similarities to some of the covenants between stronger and weaker parties from among Israel's neighbors during Moses's lifetime. Have you ever heard this suggestion before? What bearing would a study along these lines have on our interpretation of this book?

4. What are the three lenses the author outlined from Deuteronomy 28 and 30:1–10, and how do they help us make sense of the rest of the story of the Old Testament?

5. The author listed some ways that the restoration for covenant repentance was ultimately fulfilled in the person and work of Christ. Did any of these strike you as particularly glorious? Can you think of any other ways Jesus fulfilled these themes?

6. The author shared some thoughts on warnings for Christians in the book of Hebrews. Why is it important for believers in Jesus to have these warnings in their minds and on their hearts as they live the Christian life?

Conclusion

Take Up and Read!

AS THIS BOOK BEGAN, we imagined what it would be like to walk into a movie theater fifteen minutes late. We thought about trying to piece the story together without a grasp of its beginning. We observed that this would result in a nagging feeling that we were missing something, even as we watched to the end. It is impossible to fully enjoy a movie if we have missed the essential first part of the story.

Consider this book an invitation to "arrive on time" and soak in the essential first act in the Bible's grand story of redemption. I hope you have been convinced that if we are Christians who want to understand the gospel better, the Pentateuch is a great place to start. In this book we have explored some big-picture content in the Pentateuch, but the goal all along has not been to provide all the answers. The goal has been to equip readers to dive into these books on their own. Now that we have gained a better understanding of the first act in the Bible's grand storyline, I invite you to read deeply in this portion of the Bible, make your own connections to Christ and the Christian life, and soak in this glorious, life-transforming, foundational portion of God's precious word.

Bibliography

Alexander, T. Desmond. *From Paradise to the Promised Land: An Introduction to the Pentateuch*. 3rd ed. Grand Rapids, MI: Baker Academic, 2012.

Barrett, Matthew, and Ardel B. Caneday, eds. *Four Views on The Historical Adam*. Counterpoints. Edited by Stanley N. Gundry. Grand Rapids, MI: Zondervan, 2013.

Beale, G. K. *The Temple and the Church's Mission: A Biblical Theology of the Dwelling Place of God*. New Studies in Biblical Theology 17. Edited by D. A. Carson. Downers Grove, IL: InterVarsity Press, 2004.

Blackburn, W. Ross. *The God Who Makes Himself Known: The Missionary Heart of the Book of Exodus*. New Studies in Biblical Theology 28. Edited by D. A. Carson. Downers Grove, IL: InterVarsity Press, 2012.

Block, Daniel I. *Covenant: The Framework of God's Grand Plan of Redemption*. Grand Rapids, MI: Baker Academic, 2021.

———. *How I Love Your Torah, O Lord! Studies in the Book of Deuteronomy*. Eugene, OR: Wipf & Stock, 2011.

Carson, D. A. *The Gospel according to John*. Pillar New Testament Commentary. Edited by D. A. Carson. Grand Rapids, MI: Eerdmans, 1991.

Chester, Tim. *Exodus For You*. Epsom, Surrey, UK: Good Book Company, 2016.

Currid, John D. *Ancient Egypt and the Old Testament*. Grand Rapids, MI: Baker Academic, 1997.

————. "Exodus." In *A Biblical-Theological Introduction to the Old Testament: The Gospel Promised*. Edited by Miles Van Pelt. Wheaton, IL: Crossway, 2016.

Currid, John D., and David Chapman, eds. *ESV Archaeology Study Bible*. Wheaton, IL: Crossway, 2018.

Davidson, R. M. "Assurance in Judgment." *Archiv Für Religionswissenschaft* 7 (1988): 18–20.

Dempster, Stephen G. *Dominion and Dynasty: A Theology of the Hebrew Bible*. New Studies in Biblical Theology 15. Edited by D. A. Carson. Downers Grove, IL: InterVarsity Press, 2003.

DeRouchie, Jason S. "Deuteronomy." In *What the Old Testament Authors Really Cared About: A Survey of Jesus' Bible*. Edited by Jason S. DeRouchie. Grand Rapids, MI: Kregel Academic, 2013.

————. "Jesus' Bible: An Overview." In *What the Old Testament Authors Really Cared About: A Survey of Jesus' Bible*. Edited by Jason S. DeRouchie. Grand Rapids, MI: Kregel Academic, 2013.

Gentry, Peter J., and Stephen J. Wellum. *Kingdom through Covenant: A Biblical-Theological Understanding of the Covenants*. 2nd ed. Wheaton, IL: Crossway, 2018.

Glodo, Michael J. "Numbers." In *A Biblical-Theological Introduction to the Old Testament: The Gospel Promised*. Edited by Miles V. Van Pelt. Wheaton, IL: Crossway, 2016.

Greidanus, Sidney. *Preaching Christ from Genesis: Foundations for Expository Sermons*. Grand Rapids, MI: Eerdmans, 2007.

Harris, Kenneth Laing. "The Ark of the Covenant." In *ESV Study Bible*. Edited by Wayne Grudem. Accordance Electronic Edition. Wheaton, IL: Crossway, 2008.

Harris, W. Hall, ed. *NET Bible Notes*. 2nd ed. Accordance electronic edition. Garland, TX: Biblical Studies Press, 2005.

Hartley, J. E. "Day of Atonement." In *Dictionary of the Old Testament: Pentateuch*. Edited by T. Desmond Alexander and David W. Baker. Downers Grove, IL: IVP Academic, 2003.

Imes, Carmen Joy. *Bearing God's Name: Why Sinai Still Matters*. Downers Grove, IL: IVP Academic, 2019.

Mahaffey, John. "A Priest to Guide Us Home: Exodus 28–30." Sermon, May 9, 2021. West Highland Baptist Church, Hamilton, Ontario, Canada. https://www.westhighland.org/.

——. "There Is No Place Like Home: Exodus 25–27, Hebrews 9:1–14." Sermon, May 2, 2021. West Highland Baptist Church, Hamilton, Ontario, Canada. https://www.westhighland.org/.

Mendenhall, George E., and Gary A. Herion. "Covenant." In vol. 6 of *Anchor Yale Bible Dictionary*. Edited by David Noel Freedman. New York: Doubleday, 1992.

Miller, Michael. "The History of Surround Sound." *InformIT*, September 24, 2004. https://www.informit.com/.

Morales, L. Michael. *Exodus Old and New*. Essential Studies in Biblical Theology. Edited by Benjamin L. Gladd. Downers Grove, IL: IVP Academic, 2020.

——. *Who Shall Ascend the Mountain of the Lord? A Biblical Theology of the Book of Leviticus*. New Studies in Biblical Theology 37. Edited by D. A. Carson. Downers Grove, IL: InterVarsity Press, 2015.

Motyer, J. A. *The Message of Exodus*. Downers Grove, IL: IVP Academic, 2005.

——. *The Revelation of the Divine Name*. London: Tyndale, 1959.

Richter, Sandra L. *The Epic of Eden: A Christian Entry into the Old Testament*. Downers Grove, IL: IVP Academic, 2008.

Ryken, Leland, and Philip Graham Ryken, eds. *ESV Literary Study Bible*. Wheaton, IL: Crossway, 2020.

Ryken, Leland, James C. Wihoit, and Tremper Longman III, eds. "Incense." In *Dictionary of Biblical Imagery*. Downers Grove, IL: InterVarsity Press, 1998.

———, eds. "Tabernacle." In *Dictionary of Biblical Imagery*. Downers Grove, IL: InterVarsity Press, 1998.

Ryken, Philip Graham. *Exodus: Saved for God's Glory*. Preaching the Word. Wheaton, IL: Crossway, 2005.

Sailhamer, John H. *The Pentateuch as Narrative: A Biblical-Theological Commentary*. Library of Biblical Interpretation. Grand Rapids, MI: Zondervan, 1992.

Schmutzer, Andrew J. "Numbers." In *What the Old Testament Authors Really Cared About: A Survey of Jesus' Bible*. Edited by Jason S. DeRouchie. Grand Rapids, MI: Kregel Academic, 2013.

Shogren, Gary S. "Redemption: New Testament." In vol. 5 of *Anchor Yale Bible Dictionary*. Edited by David Noel Freedman. New York: Doubleday, 1992.

Steinmann, Andrew E. *Genesis*. Tyndale Old Testament Commentaries. Grand Rapids, MI: IVP Academic, 2019.

Thiessen, Matthew. *Jesus and the Forces of Death*. Grand Rapids, MI: Baker Academic, 2020.

Turner, Kenneth J. "Exodus." In *What the Old Testament Authors Really Cared About: A Survey of Jesus' Bible*. Edited by Jason S. DeRouchie. Grand Rapids, MI: Kregel Academic, 2013.

Unterman, Jeremiah. "Redemption: Old Testament." In vol. 5 of *Anchor Yale Bible Dictionary*. Edited by David Noel Freedman. New York: Doubleday, 1992.

Van Dam, C. "Priestly Clothing." In *Dictionary of the Old Testament: Pentateuch*. Edited by T. Desmond Alexander and David W. Baker. Downers Grove, IL: IVP Academic, 2003.

Vander Laan, Ray. *Echoes of His Presence: Stories of the Messiah from the People of His Day*. Colorado Springs: Focus on the Family, 1996.

Waltke, Bruce K., and Cathi J. Fredricks. *Genesis: A Commentary*. Grand Rapids, MI: Zondervan, 2001.

Waltke, Bruce K., and Charles Yu. *An Old Testament Theology: An Exegetical, Canonical, and Thematic Approach*. Grand Rapids, MI: Zondervan, 2007.

Williams, William C. "רָדַם." In vol. 3 of *New International Dictionary of Old Testament Theology and Exegesis*. Edited by Willem VanGemeren. Grand Rapids, MI: Zondervan, 1997.

General Index

Scripture Index